American Wooden

1895-1908

With an Introduction
by
Tina Skinner

Phoenix Chair Company

SHEBOYGAN   WISCONSIN

FACTORY AND WAREHOUSE:

SHEBOYGAN, WIS.

══

SALESROOM AND WAREHOUSE:

ST. ANTHONY PARK,
MINN.

1907-1908

PHOENIX
CHAIR CO.
SHEBOYGAN
WIS.

WE SELL TO
FURNITURE
DEALERS
ONLY

1907-1908

Standard Chairs and Rockers

EVENING WISCONSIN CO., CATALOGUE PRINTERS, MILWAUKEE, WIS.

Schiffer Publishing Ltd

4880 Lower Valley Road, Atglen, PA 19310 USA

Published by Schiffer Publishing Ltd.
4880 Lower Valley Road
Atglen, PA 19310
Phone: (610) 593-1777; Fax: (610) 593-2002
E-mail: Schifferbk@aol.com
Please write for a free catalog.
This book may be purchased from the publisher.
Please include $3.95 for shipping.

In Europe, Schiffer books are distributed by
Bushwood Books
84 Bushwood Lane
Kew Gardens
Surrey TW9 3BQ England
Phone: 44 (0)181 948-8119
Fax: 44 (0)181 948-3232
E-mail: Bushwd@aol.com

Please try your bookstore first.

We are interested in hearing from authors with book
ideas on related subjects.

Introduction

What better way to identify and date an item than to get the information straight from the maker?

Found intact and perfectly preserved, this treasure contains an entire line from what was once one of the largest wooden chair manufacturers in the world. Page after page details the designs and solid crafstmanship of turn-of-the-century furniture—an excellent anthology of state-of-the-art wooden wares from that era.

The catalog takes the onlooker back to a time when "Chairs, Cheese, Churches, and Children" was the motto of Sheboygan, Wisconsin. At the turn of the century, the Phoenix Chair Company rose to the top of its industry in a city, and a region, already dominated by furniture makers.

Sheboygan was a city well-suited to the furniture industry, according to *Sheboygan County: 150 Years of Progress* by Janice Hildebrand. Early settlers who made the arduous journey to the town seldom managed to bring furniture with them, thus creating a local market. Many of the new settlers were skilled craftsmen who provided their knowledge and manpower to the budding furniture industry. Plus, innovations in woodworking machinery were bringing furniture prices down into the range of middle-income families.

By 1880, oak was replacing maple as the material of choice among furniture manufacturers. Huge stands of virgin oak were being exploited in the South and Midwest. In addition, Sheboygan offered a vigorous supply of hydropower from the same-named Sheboygan River and the Pigeon River within the city, and several additional rivers in the surrounding county.

When furniture supply exceeded local demand, the city's location right on Lake Michigan made it easy to ship the newly made goods out. This was during an era of nationwide transportation innovations, with expansion of railways and highways helping to lower shipping costs. Besides bringing the boats to Sheboygan and carrying away the goods, the ships' crews were often handy craftsmen. Forced to winter in the city, they were available to handle cargo in the spring before heading out to deliver it, Hildebrand wrote.

The Phoenix Chair Company was organized in May of 1875 and employed seventy-five people. "By 1886, the factory was one of the largest and most complete," according to Nancy Schiffer, author of *America's Oak Furniture*. There were four hundred to five hundred men making furniture for Phoenix by 1888, in a plant that occupied eighteen acres of land. It maintained its momentum right up until World War I, according to Hildebrand, enjoying a boom period along with the entire furniture industry in Sheboygan. It had branches in Grand Rapids, Michigan, Chicago, and New York. In the 1930s, however, the company almost went bankrupt. It was revived through a restructuring, and sold years later, in 1957, to Milwaukee investors. In 1962, it suffered a devastating fire, and in 1963 the company president was killed in an automobile accident. A year later, in January 1964, the company closed down. The buildings were purchased and raised in 1967.

Yet there has been a "phoenix"-like resurrection of the old chair company. The golden oak furniture that was the mainstay of its early 1900s product line is enjoying "an intense revival in recent years," according to Velma Susanne Warren, author of *Golden Oak Furniture*. That same golden oak, as well as abundant elm, leant itself to fashionable bentwood designs imported from Vienna, now enjoying their second round of popularity Stateside among collectors.

The chairs, benches, and even children's seats from the Phoenix Chair Company stand in testament to a time when mighty, virgin forests made way for an innovative and prosperous new population.

The value of these pieces varies according to many different factors, making it impossible to create an absolutely accurate price list. The current-day values beside each piece are a guide to prices one could realistically expect to pay. The publisher is not responsible for any outcomes resulting from consulting this guide.

—Tina Skinner

WHERE THE FAMOUS LINE OF PHOENIX CHAIRS ARE MADE.   FACTORY, SHEBOYGAN, WIS.

FOREWORD

In presenting this, our latest Catalogue, to the Furniture Trade, it has been our endeavor to make the same thoroughly representative of the many excellent features embodied in our large line of Standard Chairs and Rockers.

It is our foremost aim to produce goods representing the highest possible type of excellence, using none but the very best material obtainable and employing skilled artisans in construction, and this, with our experience, extended over a period of thirty-five years in manufacturing, insures the production of goods in which the highest standard of excellence is embodied, and enables us to give our customers a guarantee of a class of goods superior to any in the market.

We call the attention of the dealer to our upholstered patterns, and especially to the spring work, as upon this more than on any other essential, depends the life and durability of spring upholstered chair seats. We use only the best quality of high tempered steel springs, and our steel construction as embodied in our spring seats, we know positively and assure you, stands unsurpassed in the markets to-day. Over this steel construction we place the best No. 1 leather to be obtained. It will be seen from this that the seats in our chairs are the best procurable.

The material, workmanship and finish of all our Chairs are superior to anything given for the same price, which is attested by our rapidly growing trade.

Our reputation is built on the basis of undeviating honesty in material and construction, and we spare neither effort nor expense in maintaining the high Standard of our goods.

PHOENIX CHAIR COMPANY.

$65

No. 400.

Golden Elm, Gloss.
Weight each, 9 pounds.

$65

No. 31.

Golden Elm, Gloss.
Weight each, 10 pounds.

PHOENIX CHAIR CO.
SHEBOYGAN, WIS.

$85

No. 174.

Golden Elm, Gloss.
Weight each, 9 pounds.

$75

No. 31½.

Golden Elm, Gloss.
Weight each, 10 pounds.

$65

No. 290.

Golden Elm, Gloss.
Weight each, 9 pounds.

$75

No. 290½.

Golden Elm, Gloss.
Weight each, 10 pounds.

PHOENIX CHAIR CO.
SHEBOYGAN, WIS.

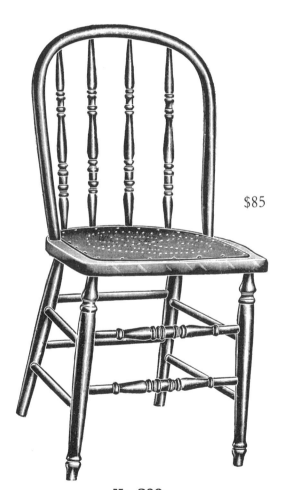

$85

No. 300.

Golden Elm, Gloss.
Weight each, 9 pounds.

$90

No. 300½.

Golden Elm, Gloss.
Weight each, 10 pounds.

PHOENIX CHAIR CO.
SHEBOYGAN, WIS,

$65

No. 109.

Diner, Tripod Construction.
Wood Seat.
Golden Elm, Gloss.
Weight each, 9 pounds.

$90

No. 109½.

Sewing Rocker.
Tripod Construction.
Wood Seat.
Golden Elm, Gloss.
Weight each, 10 pounds.

PHOENIX CHAIR CO.
SHEBOYGAN, WIS.

$75

$90

No. 110.

Diner, Tripod Construction.
Wood Seat.
Golden Elm, Gloss.
Weight each, 10 pounds.

No. 110½.

Sewing Rocker.
Tripod Construction.
Wood Seat.
Golden Elm, Gloss.
Weight each, 11 pounds.

$75

No. 112.

Diner, Tripod Construction.
Wood Seat.
Golden Elm, Gloss.
Weight each, 10 pounds.

$100

No. 112½.

Sewing Rocker, Tripod Construction.
Wood Seat.
Golden Elm, Gloss.
Weight each, 11 pounds.

PHOENIX CHAIR CO.
SHEBOYGAN, WIS,

$75

$100

No. 113.

Diner.
Wood Seat.
Golden Elm, Gloss.
Weight each, 11 pounds.

No. 113½.

Sewing Rocker.
Wood Seat.
Golden Elm, Gloss.
Weight each, 12 pounds.

PHOENIX CHAIR CO.
SHEBOYGAN, WIS.

$75

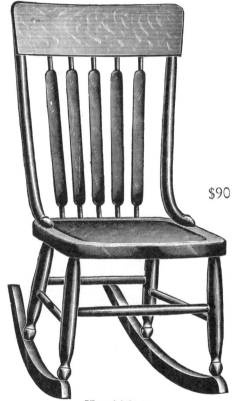

$90

No. 114.

Diner.
Wood Seat.
Golden Elm, Gloss.
Weight each, 11 pounds.

No. 114½.

Sewing Rocker.
Wood Seat.
Golden Elm, Gloss.
Weight each, 12 pounds.

PHOENIX CHAIR CO.
SHEBOYGAN, WIS.

$75

$100

No. 115.

Diner.
Wood Seat.
Golden Elm, Gloss.
Weight each, 11 pounds.

No. 115½.

Sewing Rocker.
Wood Seat.
Golden Elm, Gloss.
Weight each, 12 pounds.

PHOENIX CHAIR CO.
SHEBOYGAN, WIS.

$75

$100

No. 116.

Diner.
Wood Seat.
Golden Elm, Gloss.
Weight each, 11 pounds.

No. 116½.

Sewing Rocker.
Wood Seat.
Golden Elm, Gloss.
Weight each, 12 pounds.

$65

$90

No. 381.

Diner.
Wood Seat.
Golden Elm, Gloss.
Weight each, 12 pounds.

No. 385.

Sewing Rocker.
Wood Seat.
Golden Elm, Gloss.
Weight each, 13 pounds.

PHOENIX CHAIR CO.
SHEBOYGAN, WIS.

$65

No. 361.

Diner.
Wood Seat.
Golden Elm, Gloss.
Weight each, 12 pounds.

$90

No. 365.

Sewing Rocker.
Wood Seat.
Golden Elm, Gloss.
Weight each, 13 pounds.

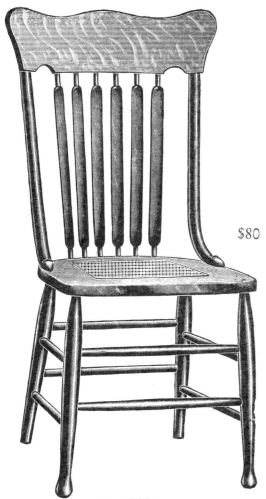

$80

$110

No. 362.

Diner.
Cane Seat.
Golden Elm, Gloss.
Weight each, 10 pounds.

No. 366.

Sewing Rocker.
Cane Seat.
Golden Elm, Gloss.
Weight each, 11 pounds.

PHŒNIX CHAIR CO.
SHEBOYGAN, WIS.

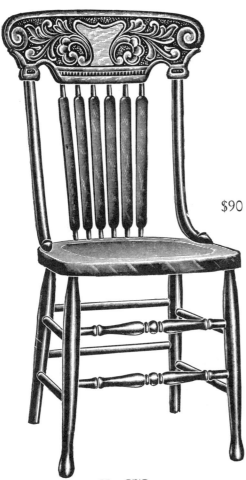

$90

No. 373.

Diner.
Wood Seat.
Golden Elm, Gloss.
Weight each, 13 pounds.

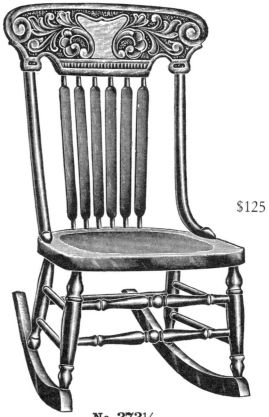

$125

No. 373½.

Sewing Rocker.
Wood Seat.
Golden Elm, Gloss.
Weight each, 15 pounds.

PHOENIX CHAIR CO.
SHEBOYGAN, WIS.

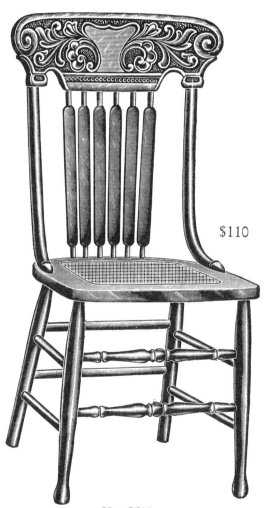

$110

No. 374.

Diner.
Cane Seat.
Golden Elm, Gloss.
Weight each, 10 pounds.

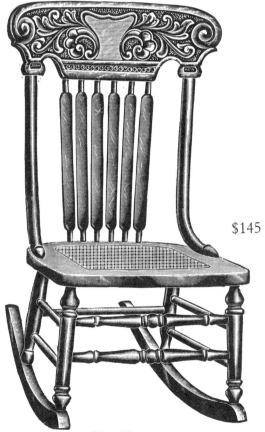

$145

No. 374½.

Sewing Rocker.
Cane Seat.
Golden Elm, Gloss.
Weight each, 11 pounds.

PHOENIX CHAIR CO.
SHEBOYGAN, WIS,

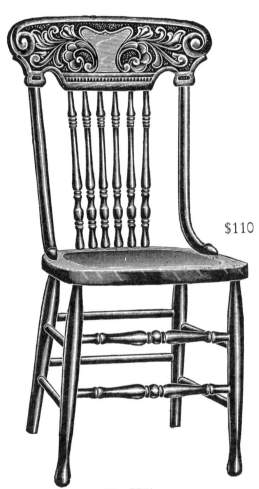

$110

No. 375.

Diner.
Wood Seat.
Golden Elm, Gloss.
Weight each, 13 pounds.

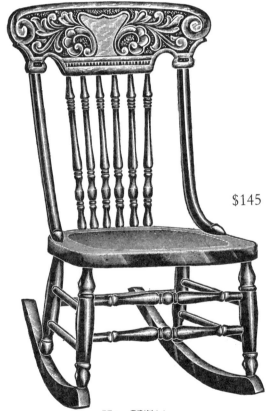

$145

No. 375½.

Sewing Rocker.
Wood Seat.
Golden Elm, Gloss.
Weight each, 15 pounds.

PHŒNIX CHAIR CO.
SHEBOYGAN, WIS.

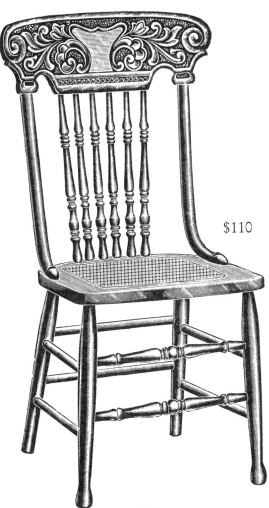

$110

No. 376.

Diner.
Cane Seat.
Golden Elm, Gloss.
Weight each, 10 pounds.

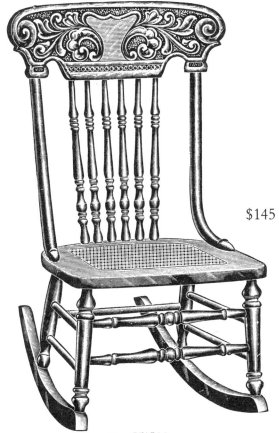

$145

No. 376½.

Sewing Rocker.
Cane Seat.
Golden Elm, Gloss.
Weight each, 11 pounds.

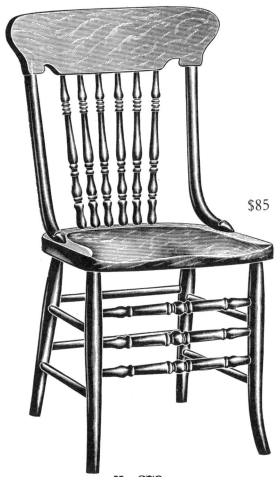

$85

No. 379.

Diner.
Wood Seat.
Golden Elm, Gloss.
Weight each, 13 pounds.

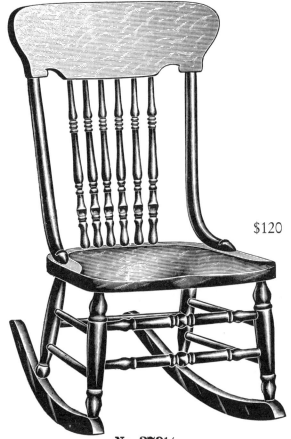

$120

No. 379½.

Sewing Rocker.
Wood Seat.
Golden Elm, Gloss.
Weight each, 15 pounds.

PHOENIX CHAIR CO.
SHEBOYGAN, WIS.

$85

$120

No. 377.

Diner.
Wood Seat.
Golden Elm, Gloss.
Weight each, 13 pounds.

No. 377½.

Sewing Rocker.
Wood Seat.
Golden Elm, Gloss.
Weight each, 15 pounds.

PHOENIX CHAIR CO.
SHEBOYGAN, WIS,

$125

$165

No. 261½.

Diner.
Wood Seat.
Golden Elm, Gloss.
Weight each, 12 pounds.

No. 265½.

Sewing Rocker.
Wood Seat.
Golden Elm, Gloss.
Weight each, 15 pounds.

No. 262½.

Diner.
Cane Seat.
Golden Elm, Gloss.
Weight each, 11 pounds.

$135

No. 266½.

Sewing Rocker.
Cane Seat.
Golden Elm, Gloss.
Weight each, 14 pounds.

$175

PHOENIX CHAIR CO.
SHEBOYGAN, WIS.

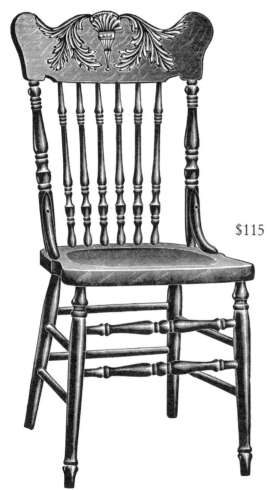

$115

No. 303½.

Diner.
Wood Seat.
Golden Elm, Gloss.
Weight each, 12 pounds.

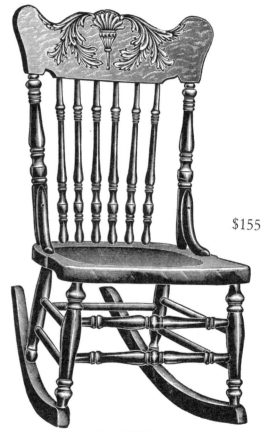

$155

No. 307½.

Sewing Rocker.
Wood Seat.
Golden Elm, Gloss.
Weight each, 15 pounds.

PHOENIX CHAIR CO.
SHEBOYGAN, WIS.

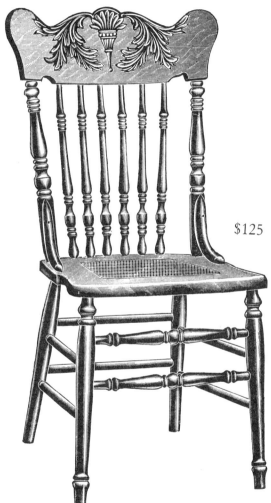

$125

No. 304½.

Diner.
Cane Seat.
Golden Elm, Gloss.
Weight each, 10 pounds.

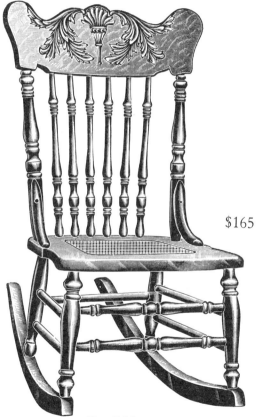

$165

No. 308½.

Sewing Rocker.
Cane Seat.
Golden Elm, Gloss.
Weight each, 13 pounds.

$80

$100

No. 420.

Diner.
Cane Seat.
Golden Elm, Gloss.
Weight each, 8 pounds.

No. 420-U.

Diner.
Upholstered Imitation Leather Seat.
Golden Elm, Gloss.
Weight each, 9 pounds.

PHOENIX CHAIR CO.
SHEBOYGAN, WIS.

$80

No. 421.

Diner.
Cane Seat.

No. 421-U. Same.

Upholstered Imitation Leather Seat.
Golden Elm, Gloss.
Weight each, 9 pounds.

$110

No. 421½.

Sewing Rocker.
Cane Seat.
Golden Elm, Gloss.
Weight each, 12 pounds.

PHOENIX CHAIR CO.
SHEBOYGAN, WIS.

$90

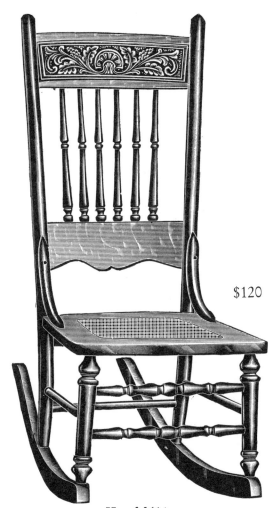

$120

No. 441.

Diner.
Cane Seat.
Golden Elm, Gloss.
Weight each, 9 pounds.

No. 441½.

Sewing Rocker.
Cane Seat.
Golden Elm, Gloss.
Weight each, 11 pounds.

PHOENIX CHAIR CO.
SHEBOYGAN, WIS.

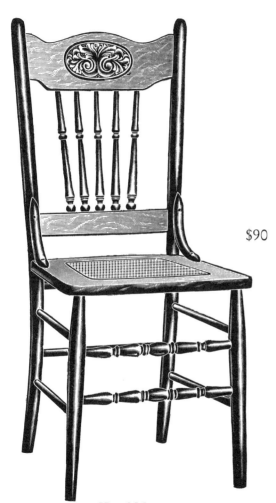

$90

No. 422.

Diner.
Cane Seat.
Golden Elm, Gloss.
Weight each, 9 pounds.

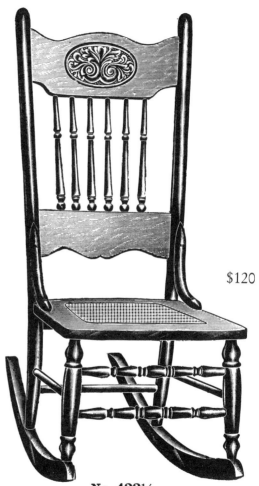

$120

No. 422½.

Sewing Rocker.
Cane Seat.
Golden Elm, Gloss.
Weight each, 11 pounds.

PHOENIX CHAIR CO.
SHEBOYGAN, WIS.

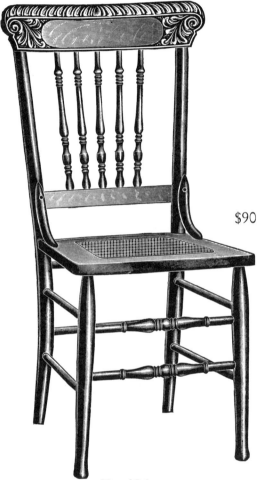

$90

$120

No. 404.

Diner.
Cane Seat.

No. 404-U. Same.
Upholstered Imitation Leather Seat.
Golden Elm, Gloss.
Golden Oak, Gloss.
Weight each, 9 pounds.

No. 404½.

Sewing Rocker.
Cane Seat.
Golden Elm, Gloss.
Golden Oak, Gloss.
Weight each, 11 pounds.

PHOENIX CHAIR CO.
SHEBOYGAN, WIS.

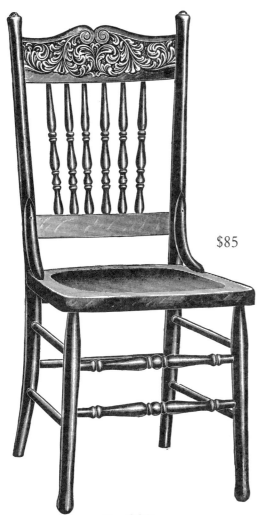

$85

No. 399.

Diner.
Wood Seat.
Golden Elm, Gloss.
Weight each, 12 pounds.

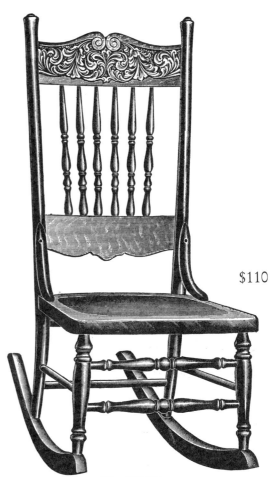

$110

No. 399½.

Sewing Rocker.
Wood Seat.
Golden Elm, Gloss.
Weight each, 14 pounds.

PHOENIX CHAIR CO.
SHEBOYGAN, WIS.

$85

No. 402.

Diner.
Cane Seat.

No. 402-U. Same.

Upholstered Imitation Leather Seat.
Golden Elm, Gloss.
Weight each, 9 pounds.

$110

No. 402½.

Sewing Rocker.
Cane Seat.
Golden Elm, Gloss.
Weight each, 12 pounds.

PHOENIX CHAIR CO.
SHEBOYGAN, WIS.

$80

No. 401.
Diner.
Wood Seat.
Golden Elm, Gloss.
Weight each, 11 pounds.

$105

No. 401½.
Sewing Rocker.
Wood Seat.
Golden Elm, Gloss.
Weight each, 14 pounds.

PHOENIX CHAIR CO.
SHEBOYGAN, WIS.

$88

No. 471.

Diner.
Wood Seat.
Golden Elm, Gloss.
Weight each, 12 pounds.

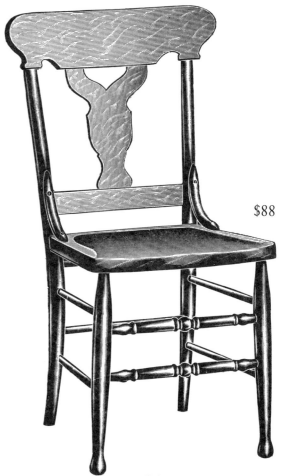

$88

No. 471½.

Diner.
Wood Seat.
Golden Elm, Gloss.
Weight each, 12 pounds.

PHOENIX CHAIR CO.
SHEBOYGAN, WIS.

$75

No. 416½.
Diner.
Wood Seat.
Golden Elm, Gloss.
Weight each, 11 pounds.

$100

No. 415.
Diner.
Wood Seat.
Golden Elm Finish, Gloss.
Weight each, 14 pounds.

PHOENIX CHAIR CO.
SHEBOYGAN, WIS.

$125

No. 151.

Diner.
Wood Seat.
Golden Elm, Gloss.
Weight each, 11 pounds.

$135

No. 152.

Diner.
Cane Seat.
Golden Elm, Gloss.
Weight each, 10 pounds.

$75

No. 161.

Diner.
Veneer Saddle Seat.
Golden Oak, Gloss.
Weight each, 9 pounds.

$95

No. 161½.

Sewing Rocker.
Veneer Saddle Seat.
Golden Oak, Gloss.
Weight each, 12 pounds.

PHOENIX CHAIR CO.
SHEBOYGAN, WIS.

$80

$110

No. 167.

Diner.
Veneer Seat.
Golden Oak, Gloss.
Weight each, 9 pounds.

No. 167½.

Sewing Rocker.
Veneer Seat.
Golden Oak, Gloss.
Weight each, 12 pounds.

PHOENIX CHAIR CO.
SHEBOYGAN, WIS.

$80

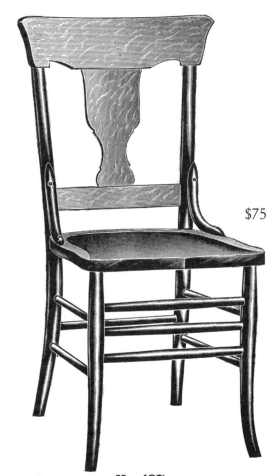

$75

No. 475.

Diner.
Veneer Seat.
Golden Oak, Gloss.
Weight each, 11 pounds.

No. 497.

Diner.
Veneer Seat.
Golden Oak, Gloss.
Weight each, 11 pounds.

PHOENIX CHAIR CO.
SHEBOYGAN, WIS.

$95

No. 660½.

Diner.
Cane Seat.
Golden Oak, Gloss.
Weight each, 12 pounds.

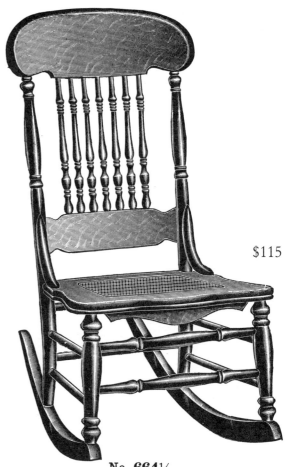

$115

No. 664½.

Sewing Rocker.
Cane Seat.
Golden Oak, Gloss.
Weight each, 14 pounds.

PHOENIX CHAIR CO.
SHEBOYGAN, WIS.

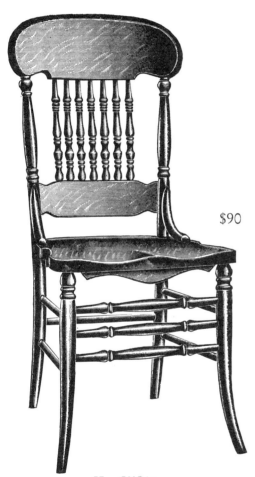

$90

No. 659½.

Diner.
Veneer Saddle Seat.
Golden Oak, Gloss.
Weight each, 11 pounds.

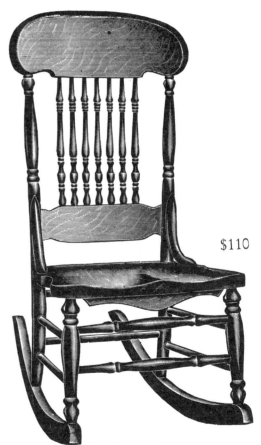

$110

No. 663½.

Sewing Rocker.
Veneer Saddle Seat.
Golden Oak, Gloss.
Weight each, 14 pounds.

PHOENIX CHAIR CO.
SHEBOYGAN, WIS.

$85

$100

No. 467.

Diner.
Veneer Saddle Seat.
Golden Oak, Gloss.
Weight each, 12 pounds.

No. 469.

Sewing Rocker.
Veneer Saddle Seat.
Golden Oak, Gloss.
Weight each, 13 pounds.

PHOENIX CHAIR CO.
SHEBOYGAN, WIS.

$90

No. 473.

Diner.
Veneer Saddle Seat.
Golden Oak, Gloss.
Weight each, 12 pounds.

$110

No. 473½.

Sewing Rocker.
Veneer Saddle Seat.
Golden Oak, Gloss.
Weight each, 15 pounds.

PHOENIX CHAIR CO.
SHEBOYGAN, WIS.

$90

No. 10.

Diner.
Wood Seat.
Golden Elm, Gloss.
Weight each, 13 pounds.

$90

No. 6.

Diner.
Wood Seat.
Golden Elm, Gloss.
Golden Oak, Gloss.
Weight each, 12 pounds.

PHOENIX CHAIR CO.
SHEBOYGAN, WIS.

$80

No. 147.
Diner.
Quartered Oak
Saddle Wood Seat.
Golden Oak, Polished.
Weight each, 14 pounds.

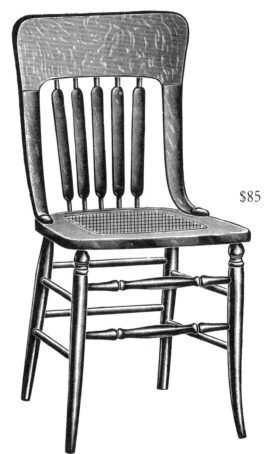

$85

No. 148.
Diner.
Cane Seat.
Golden Oak, Polished.
Weight each, 12 pounds.

PHOENIX CHAIR CO.
SHEBOYGAN, WIS.

$85

$95

No. 277.

Diner.
Veneer Saddle Seat.
Golden Oak, Polished.
Weight each, 12 pounds.

No. 278.

Diner.
Cane Seat.
Golden Oak, Polished.
Weight each, 11 pounds.

PHOENIX CHAIR CO.
SHEBOYGAN, WIS.

$85

$115

No. 278-UL.

Diner.
Upholstered Dark Olive Leather Seat.
Golden Oak, Polished.
Weight each, 12 pounds.

No. 279.

Sewing Rocker.
Veneer Saddle Seat.
Golden Oak, Polished.
Weight each, 15 pounds.

PHOENIX CHAIR CO.
SHEBOYGAN, WIS.

$52

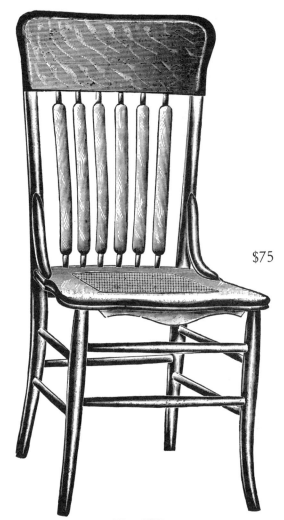

$75

No. 481.

Diner.
Veneer Saddle Seat.
Golden Oak, Polished.
Weight each, 12 pounds.

No. 482.

Diner.
Cane Seat.
Golden Oak, Polished.
Weight each, 12 pounds.

PHOENIX CHAIR CO.
SHEBOYGAN, WIS.

$80

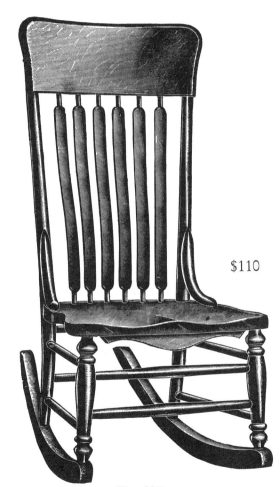

$110

No. 482-UL.

Diner.
Upholstered Dark Olive Leather Seat.
Golden Oak, Polished.
Weight each, 12 pounds.

No. 485.

Sewing Rocker.
Veneer Saddle Seat.
Golden Oak, Polished.
Weight each, 14 pounds.

PHOENIX CHAIR CO.
SHEBOYGAN, WIS.

$115

$115

No. 486.

Sewing Rocker.
Cane Seat.
Golden Oak, Polished.
Weight each, 14 pounds.

No. 280.

Sewing Rocker.
Cane Seat.
Golden Oak, Polished.
Weight each, 14 pounds.

PHOENIX CHAIR CO.
SHEBOYGAN, WIS.

$55

$60

No. 595.

Diner.
Wood Seat.
Golden Elm, Gloss.
Veneer Seat.
Golden Oak, Gloss.
Weight each, 10 pounds.

No. 409.

Diner.
Wood Seat.
Golden Elm, Gloss.
Weight each, 11 pounds.

PHOENIX CHAIR CO.
SHEBOYGAN, WIS.

$55

$60

No. 555.

Diner.
Rotary Cut Oak Veneer Seat and Back.
Golden Oak Finish, Gloss.
Weight each, 10 pounds.

No. 561.

Diner.
Rotary Cut Oak Veneer Seat and Back.
Golden Oak Finish, Gloss.
Weight each, 11 pounds.

PHOENIX CHAIR CO.
SHEBOYGAN, WIS.

$65

No. 598.

Diner.
Cane Seat.
Golden Oak, Gloss.
Weight each, 9 pounds.

$60

No. 597.

Diner.
Veneer Seat.
Golden Oak, Gloss.
Weight each, 9 pounds.

$60

$65

No. 597½.

Diner.
Solid Wood Seat.
Golden Oak, Gloss.
Weight each, 11 pounds.

No. 519½.

Diner.
Solid Wood Seat.
Golden Oak, Gloss.
Weight each, 12 pounds.

PHOENIX CHAIR CO.
SHEBOYGAN, WIS.

$75

No. 519.

Diner.
Veneer Seat.
Golden Oak, Gloss.
Weight each, 10 pounds.

$90

No. 519¼.

Arm Chair.
Veneer Seat.
Golden Oak, Gloss.
Weight each, 12 pounds.

PHOENIX CHAIR CO.
SHEBOYGAN, WIS.

$85

$100

No. 520.

Diner.
Cane Seat.

No. 520-UL. Same.

Upholstered Dark Olive Leather Seat.
Golden Oak, Gloss.
Weight each, 9 pounds.

No. 520¼.

Arm Chair, Cane Seat.
Golden Oak, Gloss.
Weight each, 12 pounds.

PHOENIX CHAIR CO.
SHEBOYGAN, WIS.

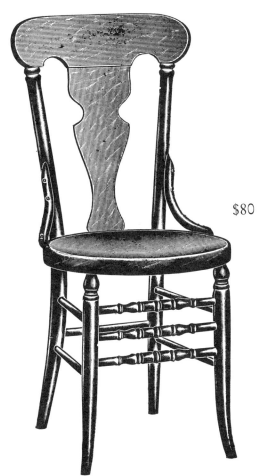

$80

No. 535½.

Diner.
Veneer Seat.
Golden Oak, Gloss.
Weight each, 11 pounds.

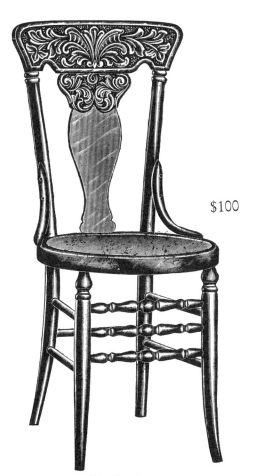

$100

No. 535.

Diner.
Veneer Seat.
Golden Oak, Gloss.
Weight each, 11 pounds.

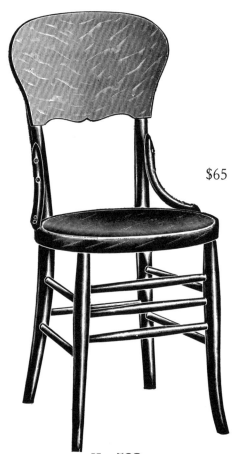

$65

$70

No. 593.

Diner.
Veneer Seat.
Golden Oak, Gloss.
Weight each, 11 pounds.

No. 591.

Diner.
Veneer Seat.
Golden Oak, Gloss.
Weight each, 11 pounds.

PHOENIX CHAIR CO.
SHEBOYGAN, WIS.

$65

No. 575.
Diner.
Veneer Seat.
Golden Oak, Gloss.
Weight each, 11 pounds.

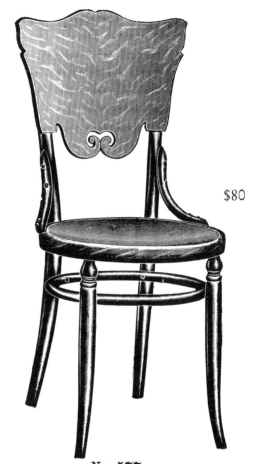

$80

No. 577.
Diner.
Veneer Seat.
Golden Oak, Gloss.
Weight each, 11 pounds.

PHOENIX CHAIR CO.
SHEBOYGAN, WIS.

$75

No. 588.

Diner.
Cane Seat.
Golden Oak, Gloss.
Weight each, 11 pounds.

$75

No. 588-UL.

Diner.
Upholstered Dark Olive Leather Seat.
Golden Oak, Gloss.
Weight each, 12 pounds.

PHOENIX CHAIR CO.
SHEBOYGAN, WIS.

$70

$95

No. 587.

Diner.
Veneer Saddle Seat.
Golden Oak, Gloss.
Weight each, 12 pounds.

No. 589.

Sewing Rocker.
Veneer Saddle Seat.
Golden Oak, Gloss.
Weight each, 12 pounds.

PHOENIX CHAIR CO.
SHEBOYGAN, WIS.

$105

$65

No. 590.

Sewing Rocker.
Cane Seat.
Golden Oak, Gloss.
Weight each, 11 pounds.

No. 575.

Diner.
Veneer Seat.
Golden Oak, Gloss.
Weight each, 11 pounds.

PHOENIX CHAIR CO.
SHEBOYGAN, WIS.

$85

$110

No. 557.

Diner.
Veneer Saddle Seat.
Golden Oak, Gloss.
Golden Oak, Polished.
Weight each, 11 pounds.

No. 559.

Arm Chair.
Veneer Saddle Seat.
Golden Oak, Gloss.
Golden Oak, Polished.
Weight each, 15 pounds.

PHOENIX CHAIR CO.
SHEBOYGAN, WIS.

$95

No. 558.

Diner.
Cane Seat.
Golden Oak, Gloss.
Golden Oak, Polished.
Weight each, 10 pounds.

$95

No. 558-UL.

Diner.
Upholstered Dark Olive Leather Seat.
Golden Oak, Gloss.
Golden Oak, Polished.
Weight each, 11 pounds.

PHOENIX CHAIR CO.
SHEBOYGAN, WIS.

$110

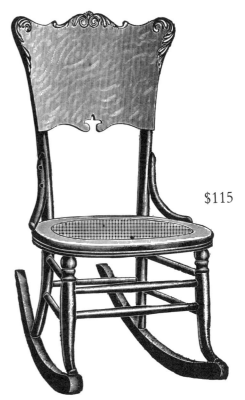

$115

No. 557½.

Sewing Rocker.
Veneer Saddle Seat.
Golden Oak, Gloss.
Weight each, 12 pounds.

No. 558½.

Sewing Rocker.
Cane Seat.
Golden Oak, Gloss.
Weight each, 12 pounds.

PHOENIX CHAIR CO.
SHEBOYGAN, WIS.

$95

No. 558-D.

Diner.
Dark Olive Leather Cobbler Seat.
Golden Oak, Gloss.
Golden Oak, Polished.
Weight each, 11 pounds.

$115

No. 558½-D.

Sewing Rocker.
Dark Olive Leather Cobbler Seat.
Golden Oak, Gloss.
Weight each, 12 pounds.

PHOENIX CHAIR CO.
SHEBOYGAN, WIS.

$100

No. 515.

Diner.
Veneer Saddle Seat.
Golden Oak, Gloss.
Weight each, 12 pounds.

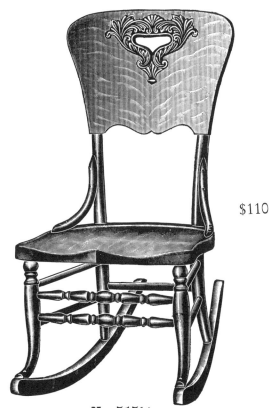

$110

No. 515½.

Sewing Rocker.
Veneer Saddle Seat.
Golden Oak, Gloss.
Weight each, 13 pounds.

PHOENIX CHAIR CO.
SHEBOYGAN, WIS.

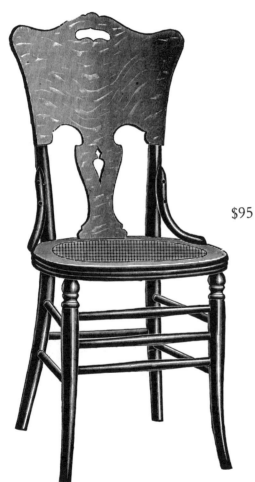

$95

No. 566.

Diner.
Cane Seat.
Golden Oak, Polished.
Weight each, 10 pounds.

$125

No. 568.

Sewing Rocker.
Cane Seat.
Mahogany Finish, Polished.
Golden Oak, Polished.
Weight each, 11 pounds.

PHOENIX CHAIR CO.
SHEBOYGAN, WIS.

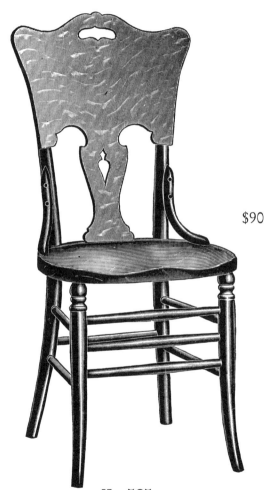

$90

$120

No. 565.

Diner.
Veneer Saddle Seat.
Golden Oak, Polished.
Weight each, 12 pounds.

No. 567.

Sewing Rocker.
Veneer Saddle Seat.
Mahogany Finish, Polished.
Golden Oak, Polished.
Weight each, 13 pounds.

PHOENIX CHAIR CO.
SHEBOYGAN, WIS.

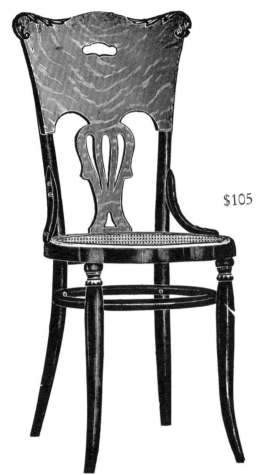

$105

$125

No. 521.

Diner.
Cane Seat.

No. 521-UL. Same.

Upholstered Dark Olive Leather Seat.
Golden Oak, Polished.
Weight each, 10 pounds.

No. 522.

Arm Chair.
Cane Seat.

No. 522-UL. Same.

Upholstered Dark Olive Leather Seat.
Golden Oak, Polished.
Weight each, 13 pounds.

PHOENIX CHAIR CO.
SHEBOYGAN, WIS.

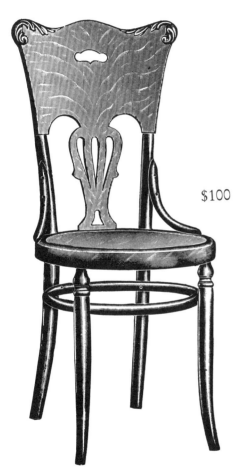

$100

No. 521½.

Diner.
Veneer Seat.
Golden Oak, Polished.
Weight each, 11 pounds.

$115

No. 522½.

Arm Chair.
Veneer Seat.
Golden Oak, Polished.
Weight each, 12 pounds.

$125

$135

No. 523½.

Sewing Rocker.
Veneer Seat.
Golden Oak, Polished.
Weight each, 11 pounds.

No. 523.

Sewing Rocker.
Cane Seat.
Golden Oak, Polished.
Weight each, 11 pounds.

PHOENIX CHAIR CO.
SHEBOYGAN, WIS.

$115

No. 526½.

Slipper Chair.
Veneer Seat.
Golden Oak, Polished.
Weight each, 8 pounds.

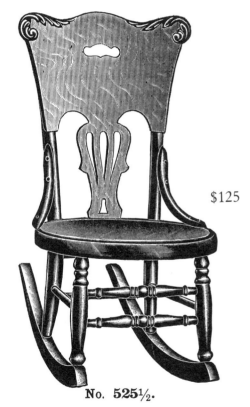

$125

No. 525½.

Slipper Rocker.
Veneer Seat.
Golden Oak, Polished.
Weight each, 10 pounds.

$115

No. 526.

Slipper Chair.
Cane Seat.
Golden Oak, Polished.
Weight each, 8 pounds.

$135

No. 525.

Slipper Rocker.
Cane Seat.
Golden Oak, Polished.
Weight each, 10 pounds.

PHOENIX CHAIR CO.
SHEBOYGAN, WIS.

$70

No. 504.

Vienna Diner.
Cane Seat.
Golden Elm, Gloss.
Mahogany Finish, Gloss.
Golden Oak, Gloss.
Weight each, 8 pounds.

$65

No. 505.

Vienna Diner.
Veneer Seat.
Golden Elm, Gloss.
Mahogany Finish, Gloss.
Golden Oak, Gloss.
Weight each, 9 pounds.

The outside dimensions of the above Chairs are:
14½ inches across arch or back.
15½ inches diameter of seat.
18½ inches height from floor to seat.
33 inches floor to top of back.

PHOENIX CHAIR CO.
SHEBOYGAN, WIS.

$70

No. 501.

Vienna Diner.
Cane Seat.
Golden Elm, Gloss.
Mahogany Finish, Polished.
Golden Oak, Polished.
Weight each, 8 pounds.

$80

No. 551.

Vienna Arm Chair.
Cane Seat.
Golden Elm, Gloss.
Mahogany Finish, Polished.
Golden Oak, Polished.
Weight each, 10 pounds.

PHOENIX CHAIR CO.
SHEBOYGAN, WIS.

$70

$75

No. 502.

Vienna Diner.
Veneer Seat.
Golden Elm, Gloss.
Mahogany Finish, Polished.
Golden Oak, Polished.
Weight each, 9 pounds.

No. 551½.

Vienna Arm Chair.
Veneer Seat.
Golden Elm, Gloss.
Mahogany Finish, Polished.
Golden Oak, Polished.
Weight each, 10 pounds.

PHOENIX CHAIR CO.
SHEBOYGAN, WIS.

$95

No. 511½.

Vienna Sewing Rocker.
Veneer Seat.
Mahogany Finish, Polished.
Golden Oak, Polished.
Weight each, 10 pounds.

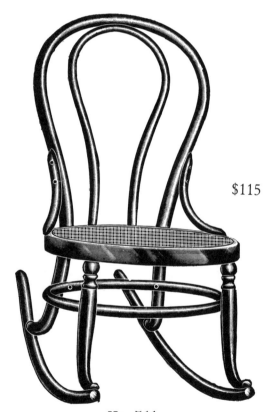

$115

No. 511.

Vienna Sewing Rocker.
Cane Seat.
Mahogany Finish, Polished.
Golden Oak, Polished.
Weight each, 10 pounds.

$75

$80

No. 503½.

Vienna Diner.
Veneer Seat.
Golden Oak, Polished.
Weight each, 9 pounds.

No. 553½.

Vienna Arm Chair.
Veneer Seat.
Golden Oak, Polished.
Weight each, 10 pounds.

PHOENIX CHAIR CO.
SHEBOYGAN, WIS.

$75

No. 503.

Vienna Diner.
Cane Seat.
Golden Oak, Polished.
Weight each, 8 pounds.

$85

No. 553.

Vienna Arm Chair.
Cane Seat.
Golden Oak, Polished.
Weight each, 10 pounds.

PHOENIX CHAIR CO.
SHEBOYGAN, WIS.

$70

$80

No. 509½.

Vienna Diner.
Veneer Seat.
Golden Oak, Polished.
Weight each, 9 pounds.

No. 510½.

Vienna Arm Chair.
Veneer Seat.
Golden Oak, Polished.
Weight each, 11 pounds.

PHOENIX CHAIR CO.
SHEBOYGAN, WIS.

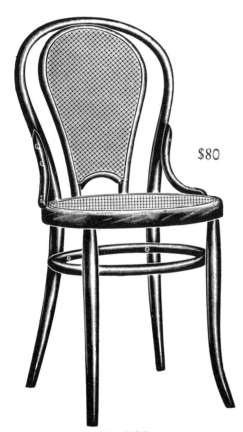

$80

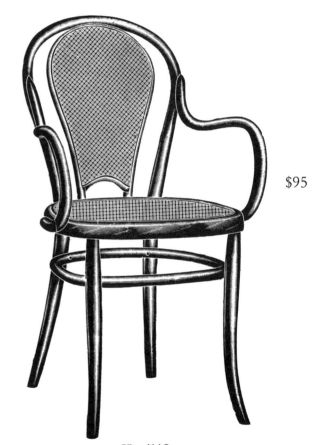

$95

No. 509.

Vienna Diner.
Cane Seat and Back.
Golden Oak, Polished.
Weight each, 10 pounds.

No. 510.

Vienna Arm Chair.
Cane Seat and Back.
Golden Oak, Polished.
Weight each, 11 pounds.

PHOENIX CHAIR CO.
SHEBOYGAN, WIS.

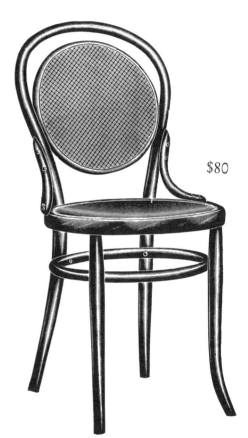

$80

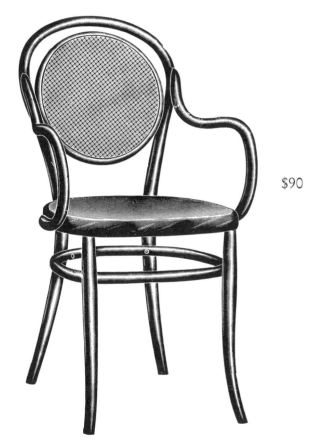

$90

No. 516½.

Vienna Diner.
Veneer Seat.
Cane Back.
Golden Oak, Polished.
Weight each, 9 pounds.

No. 517½.

Vienna Arm Chair.
Veneer Seat.
Cane Back.
Golden Oak, Polished.
Weight each, 10 pounds.

$80

No. 516.

Vienna Diner.
Cane Seat and Back.
Golden Oak, Polished.
Weight each, 9 pounds.

$95

No. 517.

Vienna Arm Chair.
Cane Seat and Back.
Golden Oak, Polished.
Weight each, 10 pounds.

PHOENIX CHAIR CO.
SHEBOYGAN, WIS.

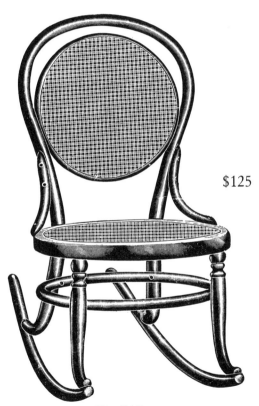

$125

No. 512.

Vienna Sewing Rocker.
Cane Seat and Back.
Mahogany Finish, Polished.
Golden Oak, Polished.
Weight each, 12 pounds.

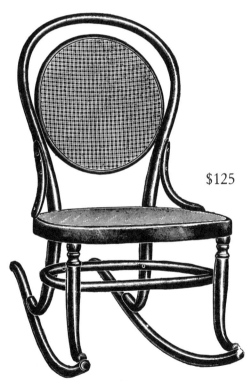

$125

No. 512½.

Vienna Sewing Rocker.
Veneer Seat and Cane Back.
Mahogany Finish, Polished.
Golden Oak, Polished.
Weight each, 12 pounds.

PHOENIX CHAIR CO.
SHEBOYGAN, WIS.

$85

$95

No. 508.

Vienna Diner.
Cane Seat.
Golden Oak, Polished.
Weight each, 10 pounds.

No. 518.

Vienna Arm Chair.
Cane Seat.
Golden Oak, Polished.
Weight each, 11 pounds.

PHOENIX CHAIR CO.
SHEBOYGAN, WIS.

$85

$105

No. 507.

Vienna Diner.
Cane Seat and Back.
Golden Oak, Polished.
Weight each, 9 pounds.

No. 514.

Vienna Arm Chair.
Cane Seat and Back.
Golden Oak, Polished.
Weight each, 11 pounds.

$75

No. 797.

Diner.
Saddle Wood Seat.
Golden Oak, Gloss.
Weight each, 12 pounds.

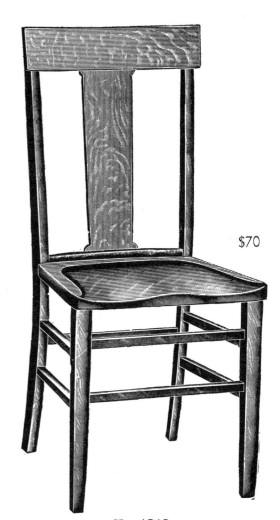

$70

No. 1210.

Diner.
Saddle Wood Seat.
Weathered Oak, Waxed.
Golden Oak, Gloss.
Weight each, 11 pounds.

PHOENIX CHAIR CO.
SHEBOYGAN, WIS.

$75

$75

No. 1214-W.

Box Seat Diner.
Quartered Oak Wood Seat.
Golden Oak, Gloss.
Weight each, 16 pounds.

No. 1214-UL.

Box Seat Diner.
Upholstered Dark Olive Leather Seat.
Golden Oak, Gloss.
Weight each, 15 pounds.

PHOENIX CHAIR CO.
SHEBOYGAN, WIS.

$80

No. 1312-W.

Box Seat Diner.
Quartered Oak Wood Seat.
Golden Oak, Gloss.
Weight each, 16 pounds.

$95

No. 1313-W.

Box Seat Arm Chair.
Quartered Oak Wood Seat.
Golden Oak, Gloss.
Weight each, 21 pounds.

PHOENIX CHAIR CO.
SHEBOYGAN, WIS.

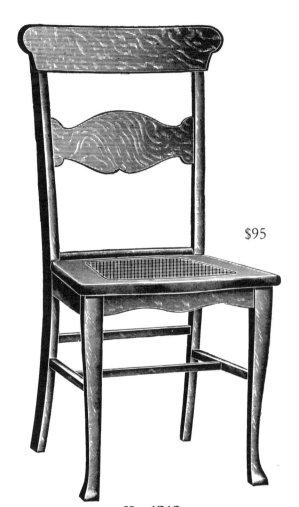

$95

$115

No. 1312.

Box Seat Diner.
Cane Seat.
Golden Oak, Gloss.
Weight each, 13 pounds.

No. 1313.

Box Seat Arm Chair.
Cane Seat.
Golden Oak, Gloss.
Weight each, 19 pounds.

PHOENIX CHAIR CO.
SHEBOYGAN, WIS.

$95

No. 1312-UL.

Box Seat Diner.
Upholstered Dark Olive Leather Seat.
Golden Oak, Gloss.
Weight each, 14 pounds.

$115

No. 1313-UL.

Box Seat Arm Chair.
Upholstered Dark Olive Leather Seat.
Golden Oak, Gloss.
Weight each, 19 pounds.

PHOENIX CHAIR CO.
"SHEBOYGAN, WIS."

$95

$115

No. 1302-W.

Box Seat Diner.
Quartered Oak Wood Seat.
Golden Oak, Polished.
Weight each, 15 pounds.

No. 1303-W.

Box Seat Arm Chair.
Quartered Oak Wood Seat.
Golden Oak, Polished.
Weight each, 20 pounds.

PHOENIX CHAIR CO.
SHEBOYGAN, WIS.

$105

No. 1302.

Box Seat Diner.
Cane Seat.
Golden Oak, Polished.
Weight each, 13 pounds.

$130

No. 1303.

Box Seat Arm Chair.
Cane Seat.
Golden Oak, Polished.
Weight each, 18 pounds.

PHOENIX CHAIR CO.
SHEBOYGAN, WIS,

$100

No. 1302-UL.

Box Seat Diner.
Upholstered Dark Olive Leather Seat.
Golden Oak, Polished.
Weight each, 14 pounds.

$125

No. 1303-UL.

Box Seat Arm Chair.
Upholstered Dark Olive Leather Seat.
Golden Oak, Polished.
Weight each, 19 pounds.

PHOENIX CHAIR CO.
SHEBOYGAN, WIS.

$100

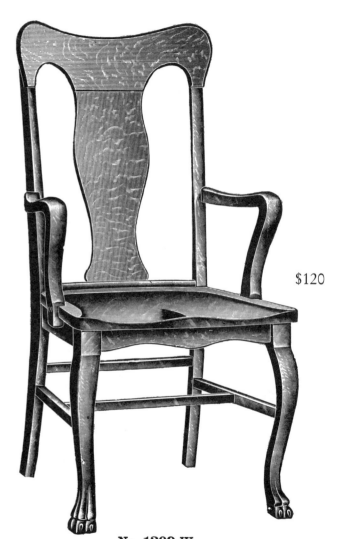

$120

No. 1308-W.

Box Seat Diner.
Quartered Oak Wood Seat.
Golden Oak, Polished.
Weight each, 15 pounds.

No. 1309-W.

Box Seat Arm Chair.
Quartered Oak Wood Seat.
Golden Oak, Polished.
Weight each, 20 pounds.

PHOENIX CHAIR CO.
SHEBOYGAN, WIS,

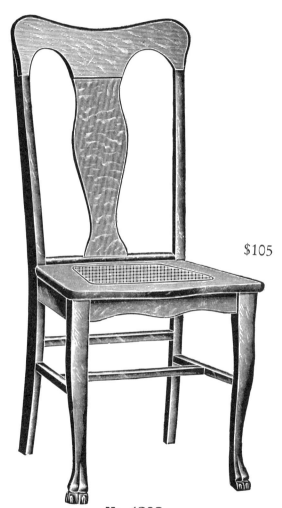

$105

No. 1308.

Box Seat Diner.
Cane Seat.
Golden Oak, Polished.
Weight each, 13 pounds.

$135

No. 1309.

Box Seat Arm Chair.
Cane Seat.
Golden Oak, Polished.
Weight each, 18 pounds,

PHOENIX CHAIR CO.
SHEBOYGAN, WIS.

$100

$125

No. 1308-UL.

Box Seat Diner.
Upholstered Dark Olive Leather Seat.
Golden Oak, Polished.
Weight each, 14 pounds.

No. 1309-UL.

Box Seat Arm Chair.
Upholstered Dark Olive Leather Seat.
Golden Oak, Polished.
Weight each, 19 pounds.

PHOENIX CHAIR CO.
SHEBOYGAN, WIS.

$100

No. 1304-W.

Box Seat Diner.
Quartered Oak Wood Seat.
Golden Oak, Polished.
Weight each, 15 pounds.

$125

No. 1305-W.

Box Seat Arm Chair.
Quartered Oak Wood Seat.
Golden Oak, Polished.
Weight each, 20 pounds.

PHOENIX CHAIR CO.
SHEBOYGAN, WIS.

$110

No. 1304.

Box Seat Diner.
Cane Seat.
Golden Oak, Polished.
Weight each, 13 pounds.

$135

No. 1305.

Box Seat Arm Chair.
Cane Seat.
Golden Oak, Polished.
Weight each, 18 pounds.

PHOENIX CHAIR CO.
SHEBOYGAN, WIS.

$105

No. 1304-UL.

Box Seat Diner.
Upholstered Dark Olive Leather Seat
Golden Oak, Polished.
Weight each, 14 pounds.

$125

No. 1305-UL.

Box Seat Arm Chair.
Upholstered Dark Olive Leather Seat.
Golden Oak, Polished.
Weight each, 19 pounds.

PHOENIX CHAIR CO.
SHEBOYGAN, WIS.

$105

$125

No. 1300-W.

Box Seat Diner.
Quartered Oak Wood Seat.
Golden Oak, Polished.
Weight each, 15 pounds.

No. 1301-W.

Box Seat Arm Chair.
Quartered Oak Wood Seat.
Golden Oak, Polished.
Weight each, 20 pounds.

PHOENIX CHAIR CO.
SHEBOYGAN, WIS.

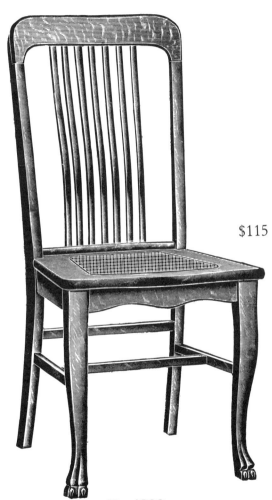

$115

No. 1300.

Box Seat Diner.
Cane Seat.
Golden Oak, Polished.
Weight each, 13 pounds.

$135

No. 1301.

Box Seat Arm Chair.
Cane Seat.
Golden Oak, Polished.
Weight each, 18 pounds.

PHOENIX CHAIR CO.
SHEBOYGAN, WIS.

$115

$135

No. 1300-UL.

Box Seat Diner.
Upholstered Dark Olive Leather Seat.
Golden Oak, Polished.
Weight each, 14 pounds.

No. 1301-UL.

Box Seat Arm Chair.
Upholstered Dark Olive Leather Seat.
Golden Oak, Polished.
Weight each, 19 pounds.

PHOENIX CHAIR CO.
SHEBOYGAN, WIS.

$70

$75

No. 1216-UL.

Box Seat Diner.
Upholstered Dark Olive Leather Seat.
Golden Oak, Polished.
Weight each, 15 pounds.

No. 1218-UL.

Box Seat Diner.
Upholstered Dark Olive Leather Seat.
Golden Oak, Polished.
Weight each, 13 pounds.

PHOENIX CHAIR CO.
SHEBOYGAN, WIS.

$85

No. 1122-HL.

Box Seat Diner.
Upholstered Dark Olive Leather Spring Seat.
Golden Oak, Polished.
Weight each, 16 pounds.

$110

No. 1123-HL.

Box Seat Arm Chair.
Upholstered Dark Olive Leather Spring Seat.
Golden Oak, Polished.
Weight each, 23 pounds.

PHOENIX CHAIR CO.

$95

$110

No. 1106-HBL.

Box Seat Diner.
Upholstered Dark Olive Leather Back and Spring Seat.
Golden Oak, Polished.
Weight each, 18 pounds

No. 1107-HBL.

Box Seat Arm Chair.
Upholstered Dark Olive Leather Back and Spring Seat.
Golden Oak, Polished.
Weight each, 23 pounds.

PHOENIX CHAIR CO.
SHEBOYGAN, WIS.

$95

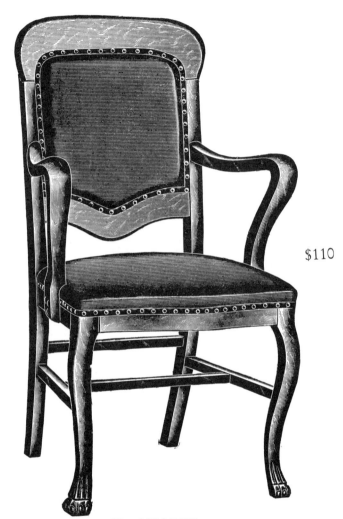

$110

No. 1130-HBL.

Box Seat Diner.
Upholstered Dark Olive Leather Back and Spring Seat.
Golden Oak, Polished.
Weight each, **17 pounds.**

No. 1131-HBL.

Box Seat Arm Chair.
Upholstered Dark Olive Leather Back and Spring Seat.
Golden Oak, Polished.
Weight each, **23 pounds.**

PHOENIX CHAIR CO.
SHEBOYGAN, WIS,

$320

No. 1134-HBL.

Settee.   Length, 40 inches.
Upholstered Dark Olive Leather Back and Spring Seat.
Mahogany Finish, Polished.
Golden Oak, Polished.
Weight each, 40 pounds.

PHOENIX CHAIR CO.
SHEBOYGAN, WIS.

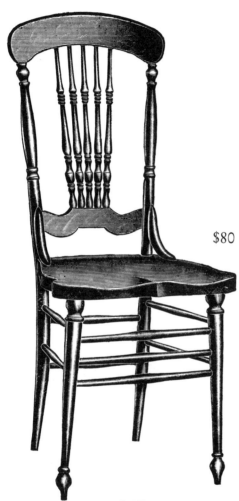

$80

No. 767.

Suite Chair.
Veneer Saddle Seat.
Mahogany Finish, Polished.
Golden Oak, Polished.
Weight each, 10 pounds.

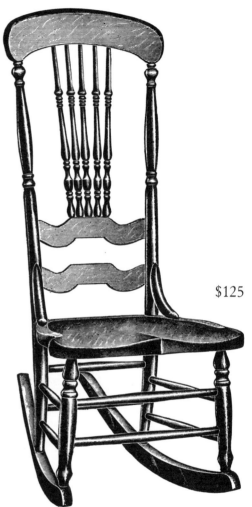

$125

No. 767½.

Suite Rocker.
Veneer Saddle Seat.
Mahogany Finish, Polished.
Golden Oak, Polished.
Weight each, 13 pounds.

PHOENIX CHAIR CO.
SHEBOYGAN, WIS.

$85

$110

No. 765.
Suite Chair.
Veneer Saddle Seat.
Mahogany Finish, Polished.
Golden Oak, Polished.
Weight each, 10 pounds.

No. 765½.
Suite Rocker.
Veneer Saddle Seat.
Mahogany Finish, Polished.
Golden Oak, Polished.
Weight each, 13 pounds.

$85

No. 763.

Suite Chair.
Veneer Saddle Seat.
Golden Oak, Polished.
Weight each, 10 pounds.

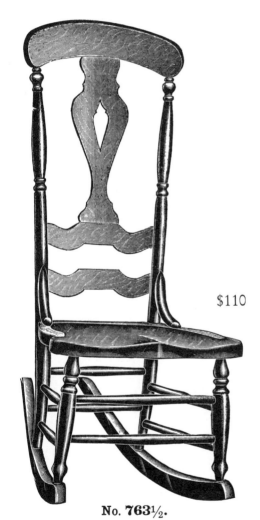

$110

No. 763½.

Suite Rocker.
Veneer Saddle Seat.
Golden Oak, Polished.
Weight each, 13 pounds.

PHOENIX CHAIR CO.
SHEBOYGAN, WIS.

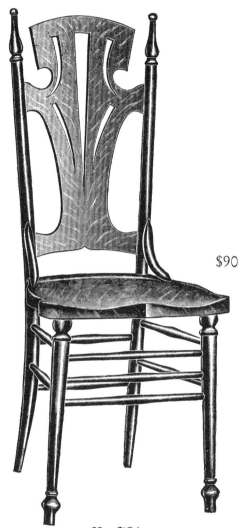

$90

No. 761.

Suite Chair.
Veneer Saddle Seat.
Mahogany Finish, Polished.
Golden Oak, Polished.
Weight each, 11 pounds.

$110

No. 761½.

Suite Rocker.
Veneer Saddle Seat.
Mahogany Finish, Polished.
Golden Oak, Polished.
Weight each, 13 pounds.

PHOENIX CHAIR CO.
SHEBOYGAN, WIS.

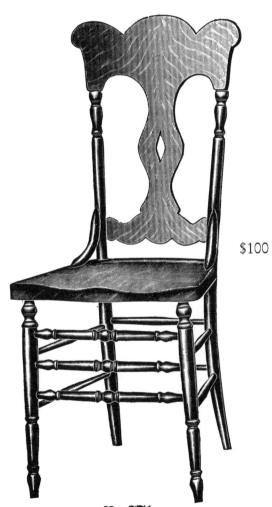

$100

No. 771.

Suite Chair.
Veneer Saddle Seat.
Golden Oak, Polished.
Weight each, 10 pounds.

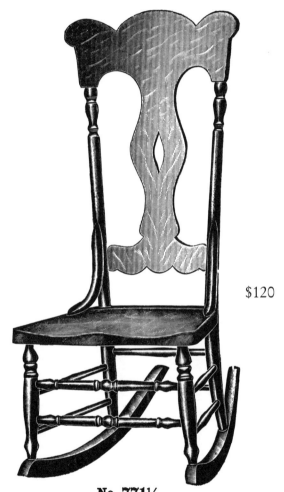

$120

No. 771½.

Suite Rocker.
Veneer Saddle Seat.
Golden Oak, Polished.
Weight each, 13 pounds.

PHOENIX CHAIR CO.
SHEBOYGAN, WIS.

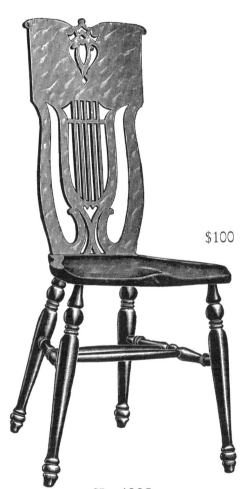

$100

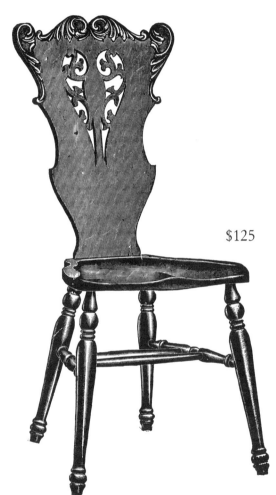

$125

No. 1002.

Hall Chair.
Veneer Saddle Seat.
Mahogany Finish, Polished.
Golden Oak, Polished.
Weight each, 12 pounds.

No. 1003.

Hall Chair.
Veneer Saddle Seat.
Mahogany Finish, Polished.
Golden Oak, Polished.
Weight each, 13 pounds.

PHOENIX CHAIR CO.
SHEBOYGAN, WIS.

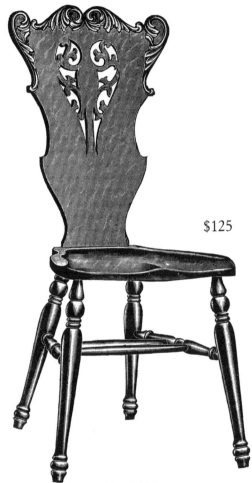

$125

$165

No. 1003.

Hall Chair.
Veneer Saddle Seat.
Mahogany Finish, Polished.
Golden Oak, Polished.
Weight each, 13 pounds.

No. 1004.

Hall Chair.
Veneer Saddle Seat.
"Faust and Marguerite" Embossed Maroon Leather Back.
Mahogany Finish, Polished.
Golden Oak, Polished.
Weight each, 13 pounds.

PHOENIX CHAIR CO.
SHEBOYGAN, WIS.

$145

$165

No. 999.

Hall Chair.
Veneer Saddle Seat.
Mahogany Finish, Polished.
Golden Oak, Polished.
Weight each, 14 pounds.

No. 1004.

Hall Chair.
Veneer Saddle Seat.
"Faust and Marguerite" Embossed Maroon Leather Back.
Mahogany Finish, Polished.
Golden Oak, Polished.
Weight each, 13 pounds.

PHOENIX CHAIR CO.
SHEBOYGAN, WIS.

$75

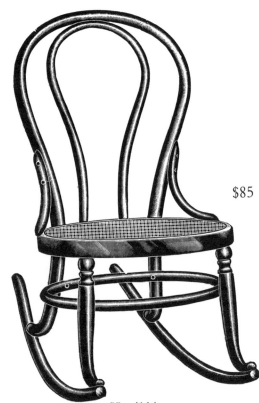

$85

No. 511½.

Vienna Sewing Rocker.
Veneer Seat.
Mahogany Finish, Polished.
Golden Oak, Polished.
Weight each, 10 pounds.

No. 511.

Vienna Sewing Rocker.
Cane Seat.
Mahogany Finish, Polished.
Golden Oak, Polished.
Weight each, 10 pounds.

PHOENIX CHAIR CO.
SHEBOYGAN, WIS.

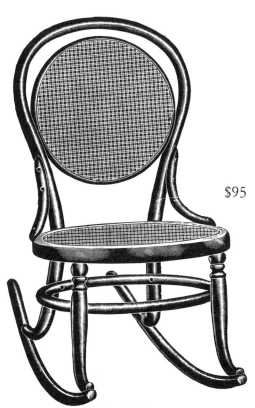

$95

No. 512.

Vienna Sewing Rocker.
Cane Seat and Back.
Mahogany Finish, Polished.
Golden Oak, Polished.
Weight each, 12 pounds.

$90

No. 512½.

Vienna Sewing Rocker.
Veneer Seat and Cane Back.
Mahogany Finish, Polished.
Golden Oak, Polished.
Weight each, 12 pounds.

PHOENIX CHAIR CO.
SHEBOYGAN, WIS.

$165

No. 957-D.

Fancy Rocker.
Fiber Cobbler Seat.
Golden Elm, Gloss.
Mahogany Finish, Gloss.
Weight each, 19 pounds.

$145

No. 419½.

Arm Rocker.
Wood Seat.
Golden Elm, Gloss.
Weight each, 20 pounds.

PHOENIX CHAIR CO.
SHEBOYGAN, WIS.

$165

No. 961.

Fancy Rocker.
Veneer Saddle Seat.
Golden Elm, Gloss.
Weight each, 20 pounds.

$165

No. 961-D.

Fancy Rocker.
Leather Cobbler Seat.
Golden Elm, Gloss.
Weight each, 20 pounds.

PHOENIX CHAIR CO.

$195

No. 960.

Fancy Rocker.
Veneer Saddle Seat.
Golden Elm, Gloss.
Weight each, 20 pounds.

$195

No. 960-D.

Fancy Rocker.
Leather Cobbler Seat.
Golden Elm, Gloss.
Weight each, 20 pounds.

PHOENIX CHAIR CO.
SHEBOYGAN, WIS.

$165

No. 673.

Arm Rocker.
Wood Seat.
Golden Elm, Gloss.
Weight each, 20 pounds.

$165

No. 674.

Arm Rocker.
Cane Seat.
Golden Elm, Gloss.
Weight each, 16 pounds.

PHOENIX CHAIR CO.
SHEBOYGAN, WIS.

$185

No. 1403.

Fancy Rocker.
Solid Wood Seat.
Rodded Arm to Seat.
Golden Elm, Gloss.
Weight each, 20 pounds.

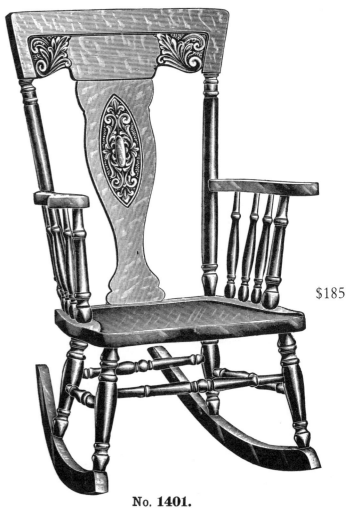

$185

No. 1401.

Fancy Rocker.
Solid Wood Seat.
Rodded Arm to Seat.
Golden Elm, Gloss.
Weight each, 20 pounds.

PHOENIX CHAIR CO.
SHEBOYGAN, WIS.

$165

No. 367.

Arm Rocker.
Wood Seat.
Golden Elm, Gloss.
Weight each, 18 pounds.

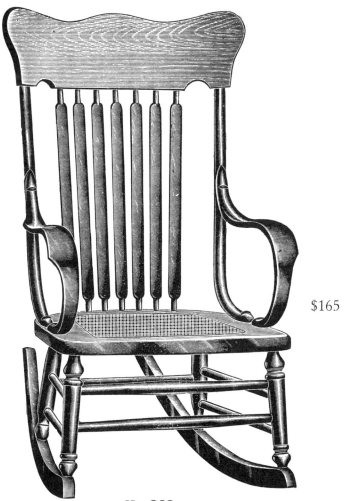

$165

No. 368.

Arm Rocker.
Cane Seat.
Golden Elm, Gloss.
Weight each, 16 pounds.

PHOENIX CHAIR CO.
SHEBOYGAN, WIS.

$195

No. 919-D.

Fancy Rocker.
Leather Cobbler Seat.
Golden Elm, Gloss.
Weight each, 21 pounds.

$195

No. 919.

Fancy Rocker.
Veneer Saddle Seat.
Golden Elm, Gloss.
Weight each, 21 pounds.

PHOENIX CHAIR CO.
SHEBOYGAN, WIS.

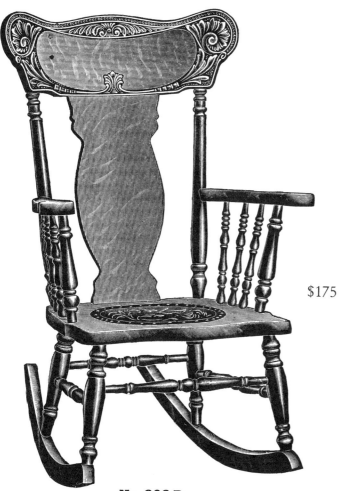

$175

No. 906-D.

Fancy Rocker.
Leather Cobbler Seat.
Golden Elm, Gloss.
Weight each, 19 pounds.

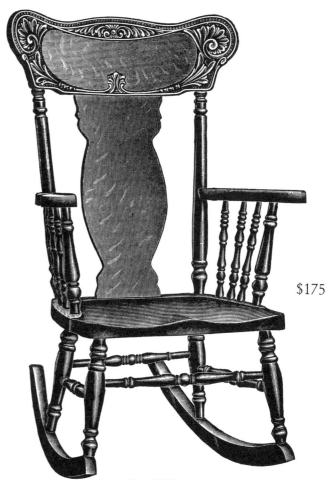

$175

No. 906.

Fancy Rocker.
Veneer Saddle Seat.
Golden Elm, Gloss.
Weight each, 20 pounds.

PHOENIX CHAIR CO.
SHEBOYGAN, WIS.

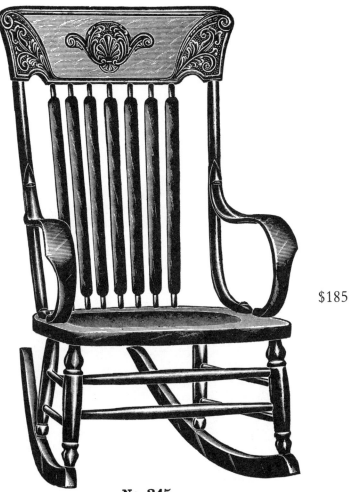

$185

No. 345.

Arm Rocker.
Wood Seat.
Golden Elm, Gloss.
Weight each, 19 pounds.

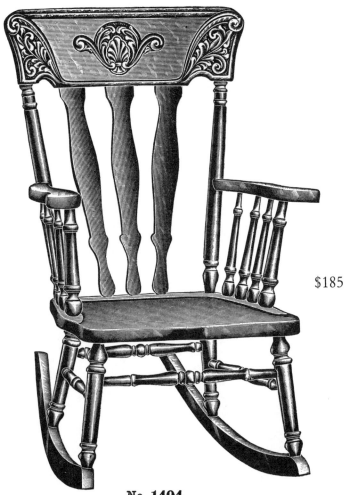

$185

No. 1404.

Fancy Rocker.
Solid Wood Seat.
Rodded Arm to Seat.
Golden Elm, Gloss.
Weight each, 20 pounds.

PHOENIX CHAIR CO.
SHEBOYGAN, WIS.

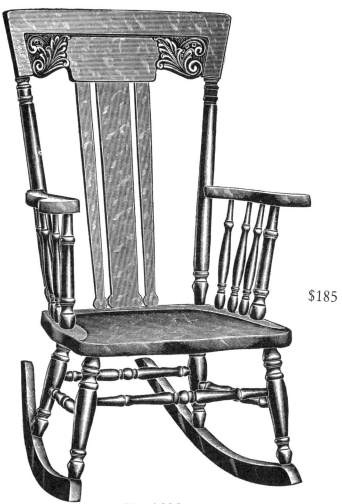

$185

No. 1402.

Fancy Rocker.
Solid Wood Seat.
Rodded Arm to Seat.
Golden Elm, Gloss.
Weight each, 20 pounds.

$220

No. 706.

Fancy Rocker.
Veneer Roll Seat.
Golden Elm, Gloss.
Rodded Arm to Seat.
Weight each, 23 pounds.

PHOENIX CHAIR CO.
SHEBOYGAN, WIS.

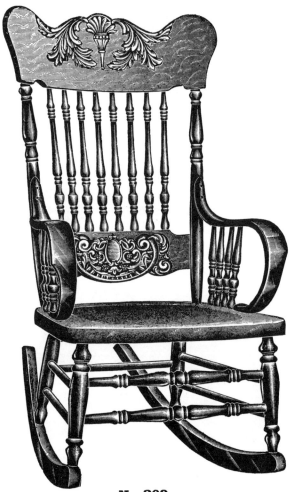

$225

No. 309.

Arm Rocker.
Wood Seat.
Golden Elm, Gloss.
Weight each, 22 pounds.

$235

No. 310.

Arm Rocker.
Cane Seat.
Golden Elm, Gloss.
Weight each, 20 pounds.

PHOENIX CHAIR CO.
SHEBOYGAN, WIS.

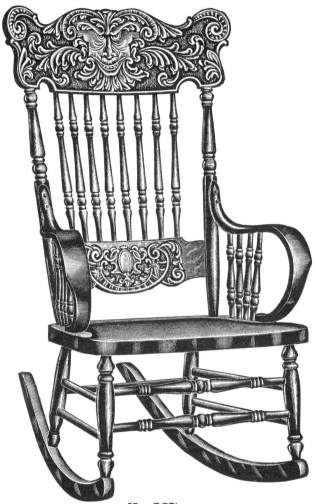

$245

No. 267.

Arm Rocker.
Wood Seat.
Golden Elm, Gloss.
Weight each, 22 pounds.

$245

No. 268.

Arm Rocker.
Cane Seat.
Golden Elm, Gloss.
Weight each, 20 pounds.

PHOENIX CHAIR CO.
SHEBOYGAN, WIS.

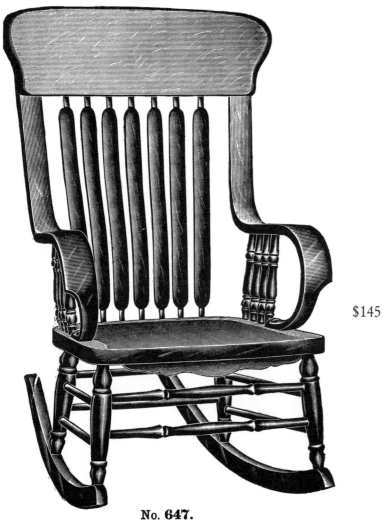

$145

$145

No. 647.

Large Arm Rocker.
Wood Seat.
Rodded Arm to Seat.
Golden Elm, Gloss.
Weight each, 26 pounds.

No. 649.

Large Arm Rocker.
Saddle Wood Seat.
Rodded Arm to Seat.
Golden Elm, Gloss.
Weight each, 26 pounds.

PHOENIX CHAIR CO.
SHEBOYGAN, WIS.

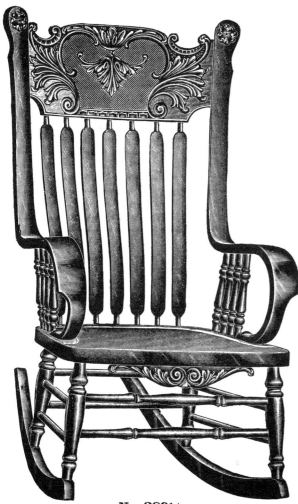

$195

$195

No. 389½.

Large Arm Rocker.
Wood Seat.
Rodded Arm to Seat.
Golden Elm, Gloss.
Weight each, 25 pounds.

No. 389.

Large Arm Rocker.
Saddle Wood Seat.
Rodded Arm to Seat.
Golden Elm, Gloss.
Weight each, 25 pounds.

PHOENIX CHAIR CO.
SHEBOYGAN, WIS.

$195

$195

No. 233.

Large Arm Rocker.
Wood Seat.
Rodded Arm to Seat.
Golden Elm, Gloss.
Weight each, 27 pounds.

No. 233½.

Large Arm Rocker.
Saddle Wood Seat.
Rodded Arm to Seat.
Golden Elm, Gloss.
Weight each, 27 pounds.

PHOENIX CHAIR CO.
SHEBOYGAN, WIS.

$195

No. 234.

Large Arm Rocker.
Cane Seat.
Rodded Arm to Seat.
Golden Elm, Gloss.
Weight each, 25 pounds.

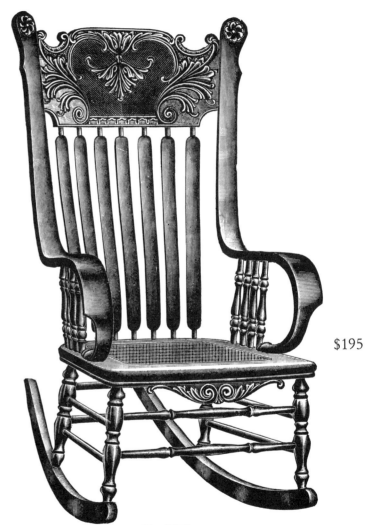

$195

No. 390.

Large Arm Rocker.
Cane Seat.
Rodded Arm to Seat.
Golden Elm, Gloss.
Weight each, 22 pounds.

PHOENIX CHAIR CO.
SHEBOYGAN, WIS.

$195

No. 390-D.

Large Arm Rocker.
Dark Olive Leather Cobbler Seat.
Rodded Arm to Seat.
Golden Elm, Gloss.
Weight each, 22 pounds.

$195

No. 234-D.

Large Arm Rocker.
Dark Olive Leather Cobbler Seat.
Rodded Arm to Seat.
Golden Elm, Gloss.
Weight each, 25 pounds.

PHOENIX CHAIR CO.
SHEBOYGAN, WIS,

$195

No. 930.

Fancy Rocker.
Veneer Saddle Seat.
Golden Oak, Gloss.
Weight each, 19 pounds.

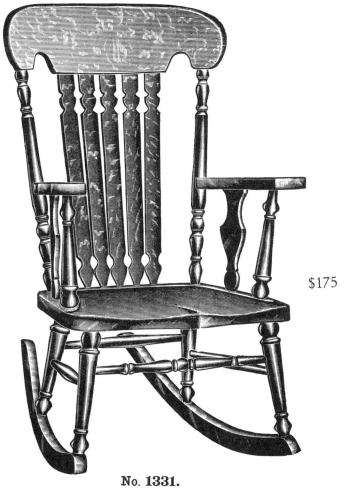

$175

No. 1331.

Fancy Rocker.
Veneer Saddle Seat.
Golden Oak, Gloss.
Weight each, 22 pounds.

PHOENIX CHAIR CO.
SHEBOYGAN, WIS.

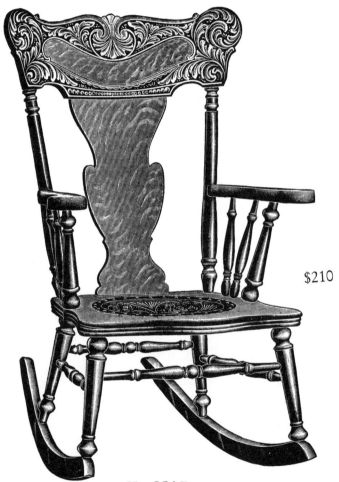

$210

$210

No. 931-D.

Fancy Rocker.
Dark Olive Leather Cobbler Seat.
Golden Oak, Gloss.
Weight each, 20 pounds.

No. 931.

Fancy Rocker.
Veneer Saddle Seat.
Golden Oak, Gloss.
Weight each, 20 pounds.

PHOENIX CHAIR CO.
SHEBOYGAN, WIS.

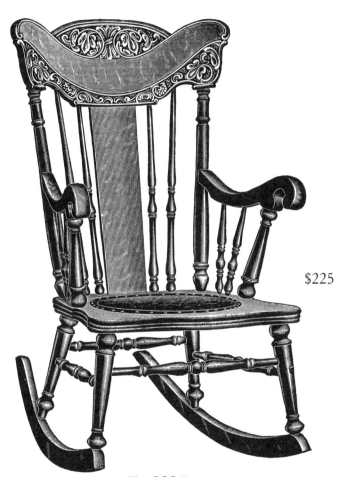

$225

No. 902-D.

Fancy Rocker.
Dark Olive Leather Cobbler Seat.
Golden Oak, Gloss.
Weight each, 20 pounds.

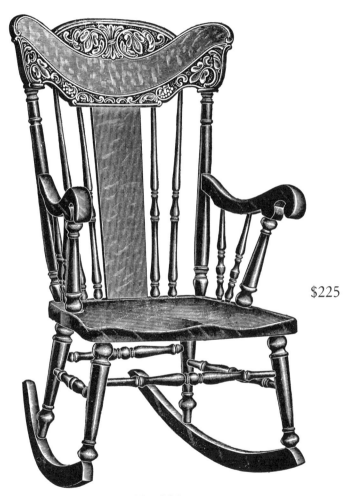

$225

No. 902.

Fancy Rocker.
Veneer Saddle Seat.
Golden Oak, Gloss.
Weight each, 20 pounds.

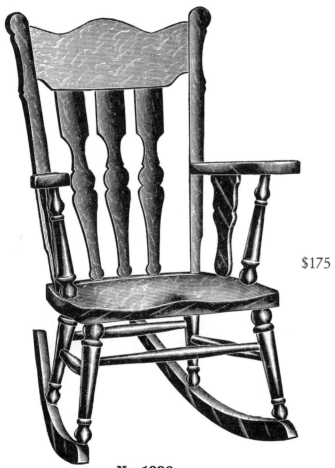

$175

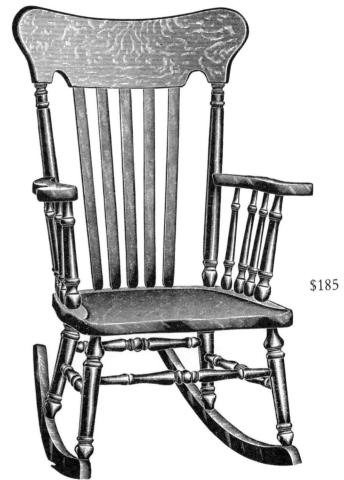

$185

No. 1090.

Fancy Rocker.
Veneer Saddle Seat.
Golden Oak, Gloss.
Weight each, 18 pounds.

No. 1089.

Fancy Rocker.
Quartered Oak Saddle Wood Seat.
Golden Oak, Gloss.
Weight each, 20 pounds.

PHOENIX CHAIR CO.
SHEBOYGAN, WIS.

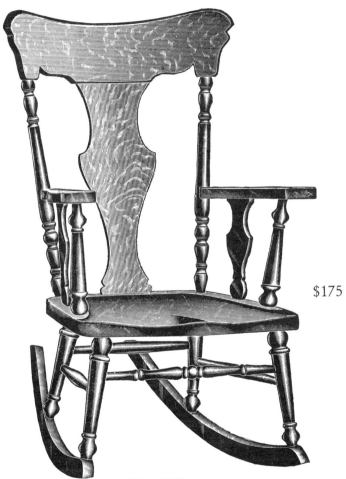

$175

No. 1332.

Fancy Rocker.
Veneer Saddle Seat.
Golden Oak, Gloss.
Weight each, 22 pounds.

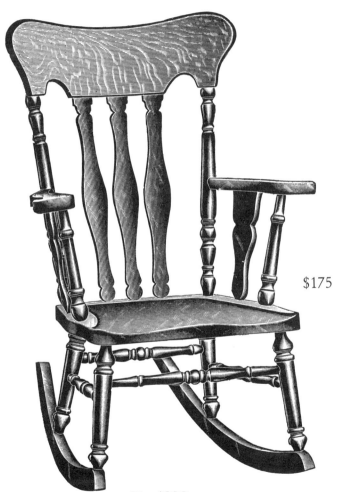

$175

No. 1092.

Fancy Rocker.
Quartered Oak Saddle Wood Seat.
Golden Oak, Gloss.
Weight each, 20 pounds.

PHOENIX CHAIR CO.
SHEBOYGAN, WIS,

$190

$190

No. 665½.

Fancy Rocker.
Veneer Saddle Seat.
Golden Oak, Gloss.
Weight each, 22 pounds.

No. 666½.

Fancy Rocker.
Cane Seat.
Golden Oak, Gloss.
Weight each, 22 pounds.

PHOENIX CHAIR CO.
SHEBOYGAN, WIS.

$220

No. 693½.

Fancy Rocker.
Veneer Saddle Seat.
Golden Oak, Gloss.
Weight each, 24 pounds.

$220

No. 694½.

Fancy Rocker.
Cane Seat.
Golden Oak, Gloss.
Weight each, 23 pounds.

PHOENIX CHAIR CO.
SHEBOYGAN, WIS.

$235

No. 693.

Fancy Rocker.
Veneer Saddle Seat.
Golden Oak, Gloss.
Weight each, 24 pounds.

$235

No. 694.

Fancy Rocker.
Cane Seat.
Golden Oak, Gloss.
Weight each, 23 pounds.

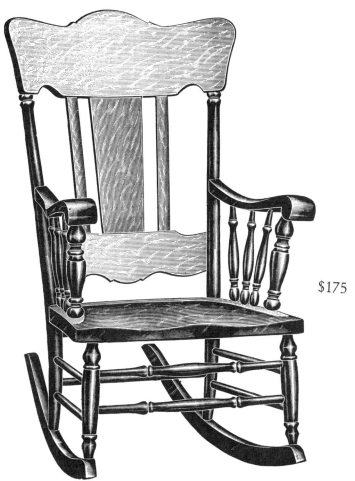

$175

$175

No. 695.

Large Arm Rocker.
Veneer Saddle Seat.
Golden Oak, Gloss.
Weight each, 23 pounds.

No. 697.

Large Arm Rocker.
Veneer Saddle Seat.
Golden Oak, Gloss.
Weight each, 23 pounds.

PHOENIX CHAIR CO.
SHEBOYGAN, WIS.

$255

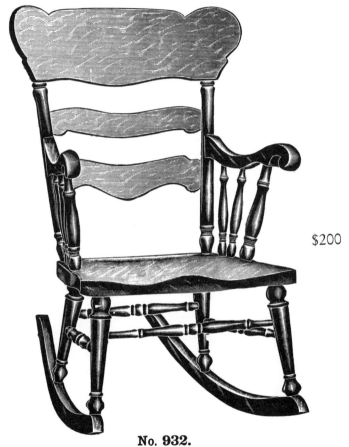

$200

No. 717.

Fancy Rocker.
Veneer Roll Seat.
Rodded Arm to Seat.
Golden Oak, Gloss.
Weight each, 23 pounds.

No. 932.

Fancy Arm Rocker.
Veneer Saddle Seat.
Mahogany Finish, Polished.
Golden Oak, Polished.
Weight each, 20 pounds.

PHOENIX CHAIR CO.
SHEBOYGAN, WIS.

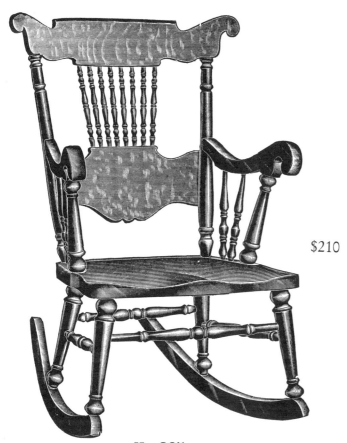

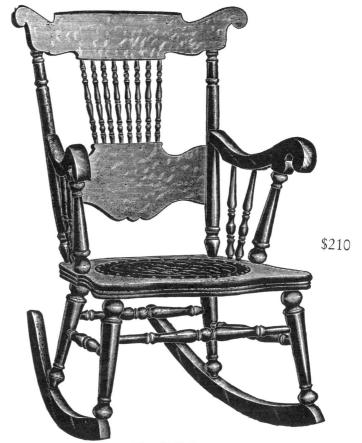

$210

$210

No. 905.

Fancy Rocker.
Veneer Saddle Seat.
Rodded Arm to Seat.
Golden Oak, Polished.
Weight each, 20 pounds.

No. 905-D.

Fancy Rocker.
Dark Olive Leather Cobbler Seat.
Rodded Arm to Seat.
Golden Oak, Polished.
Weight each, 20 pounds.

$190

$190

No. 901.

Fancy Rocker.
Veneer Saddle Seat.
Mahogany Finish, Polished.
Golden Oak, Polished.
Weight each, 18 pounds.

No. 901-D.

Fancy Rocker.
Dark Olive Leather Cobbler Seat.
Mahogany Finish, Polished.
Golden Oak, Polished.
Weight each, 18 pounds.

PHOENIX CHAIR CO.
SHEBOYGAN, WIS.

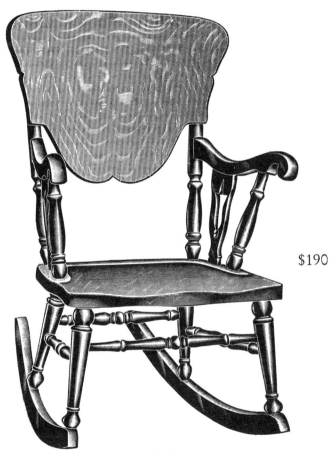

$190

No. 1088.

Fancy Rocker.
Veneer Saddle Seat.
Rodded Arm to Seat.
Golden Oak, Polished.
Weight each, 20 pounds.

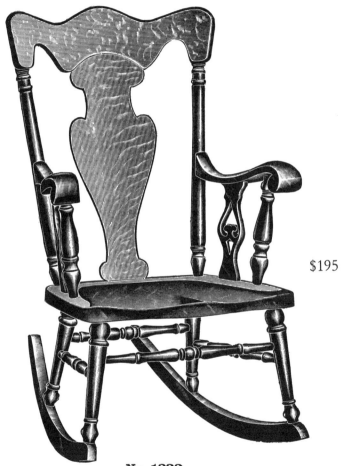

$195

No. 1333.

Fancy Rocker.
Veneer Saddle Seat.
Golden Oak, Polished.
Weight each, 20 pounds.

PHOENIX CHAIR CO.
SHEBOYGAN, WIS.

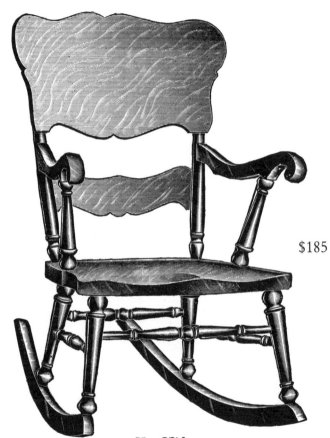

$185

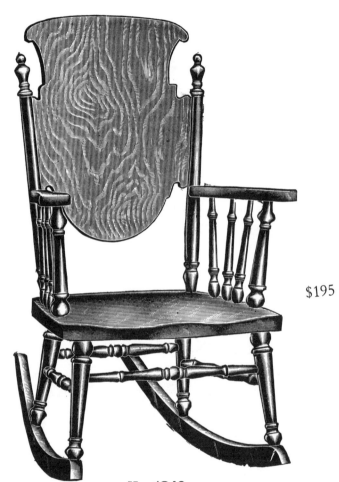

$195

No. 974.
Fancy Rocker.
Veneer Saddle Seat.
Rodded Arm to Seat.
Mahogany Finish, Polished.
Golden Oak, Polished.
Weight each, 21 pounds.

No. 1340.
Fancy Rocker.
Rotary Cut Oak, Veneer Seat and Back.
Golden Oak Finish, Polished.
Weight each, 22 pounds.

PHOENIX CHAIR CO.
SHEBOYGAN, WIS.

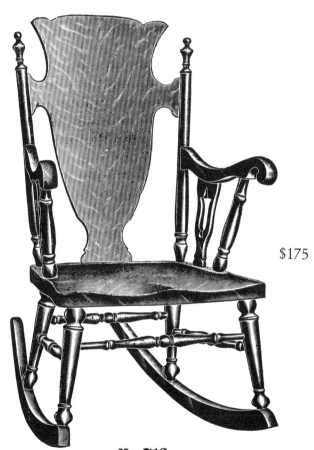

$175

No. 712.

Fancy Rocker.
Veneer Saddle Seat.
Rodded Arm to Seat.
Mahogany Finish, Polished.
Golden Oak, Polished.
Weight each, 20 pounds.

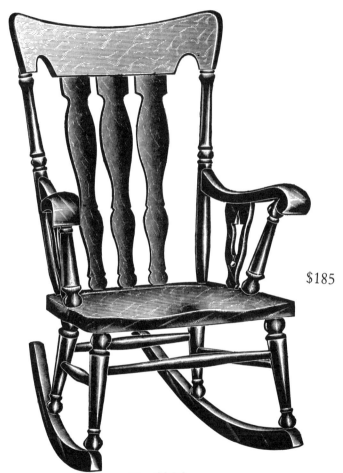

$185

No. 1084.

Fancy Rocker.
Veneer Saddle Seat.
Golden Oak, Polished.
Weight each, 20 pounds.

PHOENIX CHAIR CO.
SHEBOYGAN, WIS.

$185

No. 487.

Fancy Rocker.
Veneer Saddle Seat.
Golden Oak, Polished.
Weight each, 21 pounds.

$195

No. 488.

Fancy Rocker.
Cane Seat.
Golden Oak, Polished.
Weight each, 20 pounds.

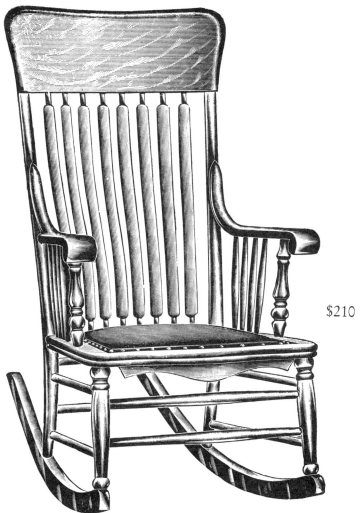

$210

No. 488-UL.

Fancy Rocker.
Upholstered Dark Olive Leather Seat.
Golden Oak, Polished.
Weight each, 21 pounds.

$200

No. 1156.

Fancy Rocker.
Veneer Saddle Seat.
Golden Oak, Polished.
Weight each, 21 pounds.

$220

No. 283.

Arm Rocker.
Veneer Saddle Seat.
Golden Oak, Polished.
Weight each, 22 pounds.

$225

No. 284.

Arm Rocker.
Cane Seat.
Golden Oak, Polished.
Weight each, 21 pounds.

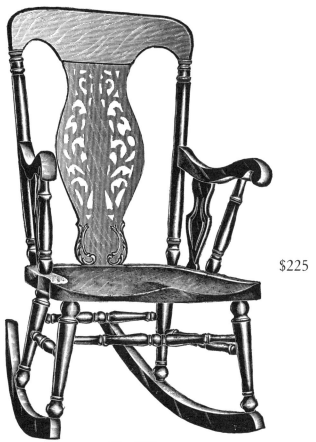

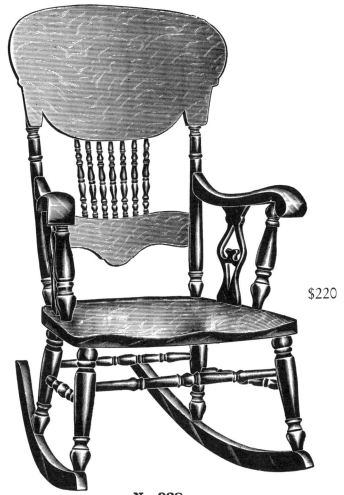

$225

$220

No. 978.

Fancy Rocker.
Quartered Oak Saddle Wood Seat.

No. 978-D. Same.

Dark Olive Leather Cobbler Seat.
Rodded Arm to Seat.
Golden Oak, Polished.
Weight each, 25 pounds.

No. 928.

Fancy Rocker.
Veneer Saddle Seat.
Golden Oak, Polished.
Weight each, 21 pounds.

PHOENIX CHAIR CO.
SHEBOYGAN, WIS.

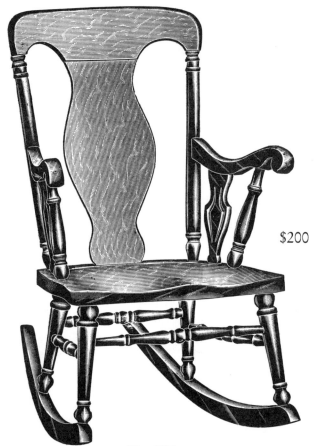

$200

No. 981.

Fancy Rocker.
Veneer Saddle Seat.
Rodded Arm to Seat.
Golden Oak, Polished.
Weight each, 18 pounds.

$220

No. 976.

Fancy Rocker.
Quartered Oak Saddle Wood Seat.

No. 976-D. Same.

Dark Olive Leather Cobbler Seat.
Rodded Arm to Seat.
Golden Oak, Polished.
Weight each, 25 pounds.

PHOENIX CHAIR CO.
SHEBOYGAN, WIS.

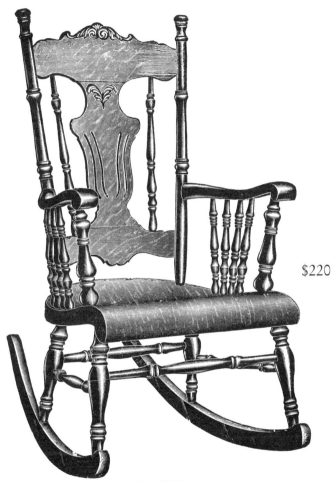

$220

No. 719.

Fancy Rocker.
Veneer Roll Seat.
Rodded Arm to Seat.
Golden Oak, Polished.
Weight each, 22 pounds.

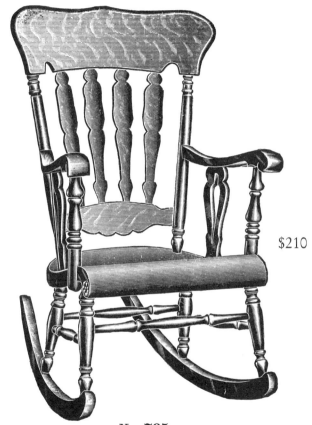

$210

No. 705.

Fancy Rocker.
Veneer Roll Seat.
Rodded Arm to Seat.
Golden Oak, Polished.
Weight each, 22 pounds.

PHOENIX CHAIR CO.
SHEBOYGAN, WIS.

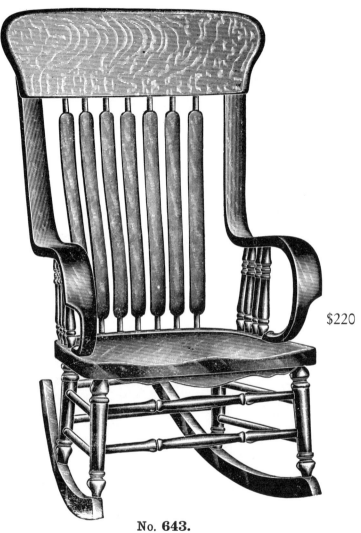

$220

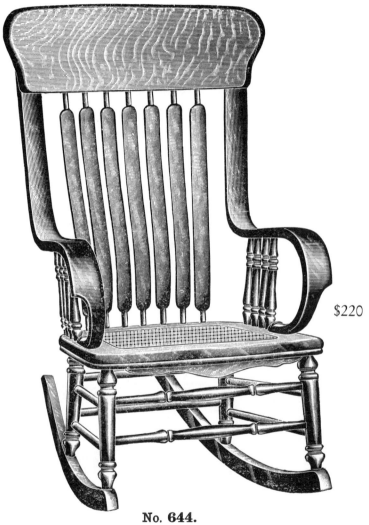

$220

No. 643.

Large Arm Rocker.
Veneer Saddle Seat.
Rodded Arm to Seat.
Golden Oak, Polished.
Weight each, 27 pounds.

No. 644.

Large Arm Rocker.
Cane Seat.
Rodded Arm to Seat.
Golden Oak, Polished.
Weight each, 25 pounds.

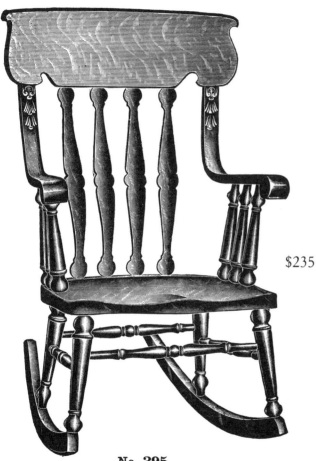

$235

No. 395.

Fancy Rocker.
Veneer Saddle Seat.
Rodded Arm to Seat.
Golden Oak, Polished.
Weight each, 27 pounds.

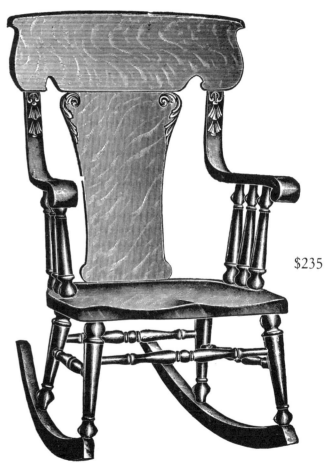

$235

No. 396.

Fancy Rocker.
Veneer Saddle Seat.
Rodded Arm to Seat.
Golden Oak, Polished.
Weight each, 27 pounds.

PHOENIX CHAIR CO.
SHEBOYGAN, WIS.

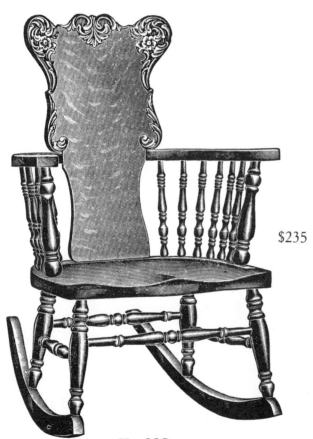

$235

No. 998.

Fancy Rocker.
Veneer Saddle Seat.
Mahogany Finish, Polished.
Golden Oak, Polished.
Weight each, 20 pounds.

$235

No. 998-D.

Fancy Rocker.
Dark Olive Leather Cobbler Seat.
Mahogany Finish, Polished.
Golden Oak, Polished.
Weight each, 20 pounds.

PHOENIX CHAIR CO.
SHEBOYGAN, WIS.

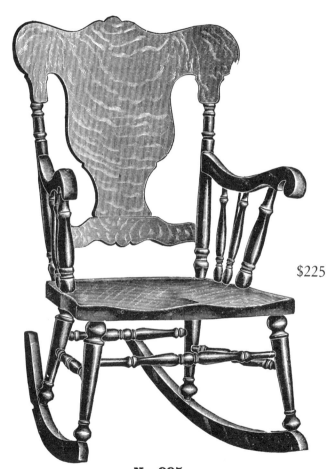

$225

No. 995.

Fancy Rocker.
Veneer Saddle Seat.
Rodded Arm to Seat.
Golden Oak, Polished.
Weight each, 20 pounds.

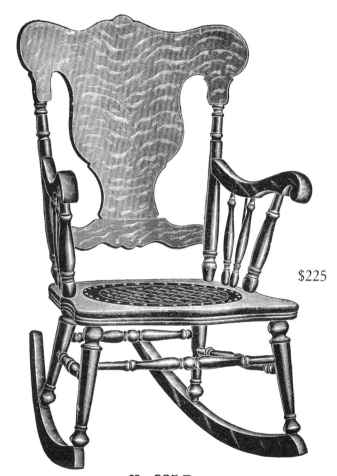

$225

No. 995-D.

Fancy Rocker.
Dark Olive Leather Cobbler Seat.
Rodded Arm to Seat.
Golden Oak, Polished.
Weight each, 20 pounds.

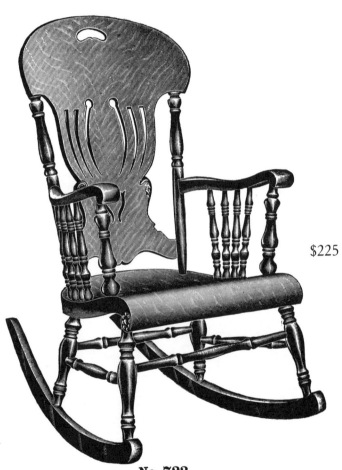

$225

No. 722.

Fancy Rocker.
Veneer Roll Seat.
Golden Oak, Polished.
Weight each, 23 pounds.

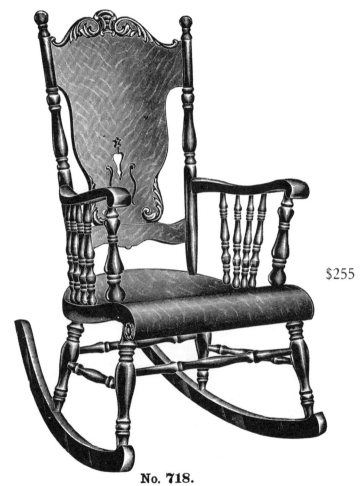

$255

No. 718.

Fancy Rocker.
Veneer Roll Seat.
Rodded Arm to Seat.
Golden Oak, Polished.
Weight each, 23 pounds.

$255

No. 985.

Fancy Rocker.
Veneer Saddle Seat.
Mahogany Finish, Polished.
Golden Oak, Polished.
Weight each, **22** pounds.

$255

No. 985-D.

Fancy Rocker.
Dark Olive Leather Cobbler Seat.
Mahogany Finish, Polished.
Golden Oak, Polished.
Weight each, 22 pounds.

PHOENIX CHAIR CO.
SHEBOYGAN, WIS.

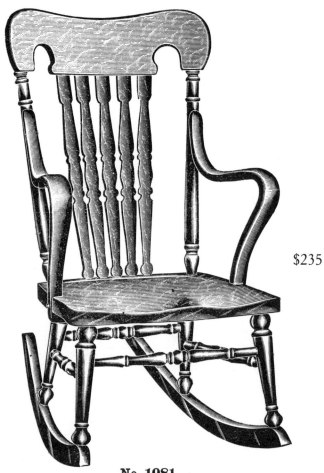

$235

No. 1081.

Fancy Rocker.
Veneer Saddle Seat.
Golden Oak, Polished.
Weight each, 18 pounds.

$235

No. 1086.

Fancy Rocker.
Veneer Saddle Seat.
Mahogany Finish, Polished.
Golden Oak, Polished.
Weight each, 18 pounds.

PHOENIX CHAIR CO.
SHEBOYGAN, WIS.

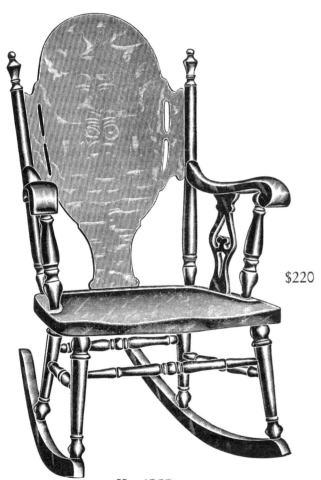

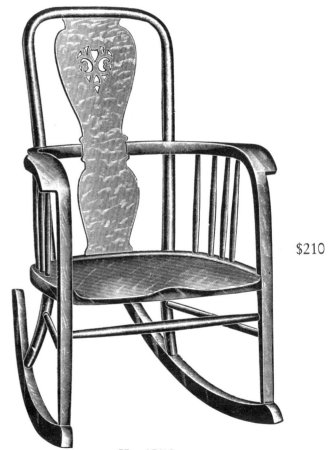

$220

$210

No. 1337.

Fancy Rocker.
Veneer Saddle Seat.
Golden Oak, Polished.
Weight each, 20 pounds.

No. 1350.

Fancy Rocker.
Quarter Sawed Oak Saddle Wood Seat.
Golden Oak, Polished.
Weight each, 20 pounds.

PHOENIX CHAIR CO.
SHEBOYGAN, WIS.

$310

No. 953-B.

Settee.
Veneer Seat.
20½ in. Height of Back.
39 in. Between Arms.
Mahogany Finish, Polished.
Golden Oak, Polished.
Weight each, 30 pounds.

$175

No. 951½.

Parlor Chair.
Veneer Saddle Seat.
Mahogany Finish, Polished.
Golden Oak, Polished.
Weight each, 16 pounds.

$250

No. 951.

Fancy Rocker.
Veneer Saddle Seat.
Mahogany Finish, Polished.
Golden Oak, Polished.
Weight each, 17 pounds.

PHOENIX CHAIR CO.
SHEBOYGAN, WIS.

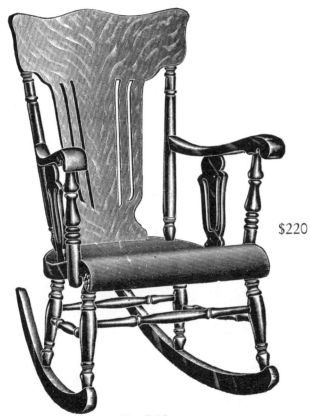

$220

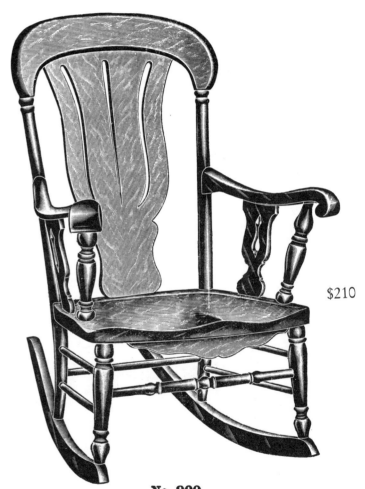

$210

No. 716.

Fancy Rocker.
Veneer Roll Seat.
Rodded Arm to Seat.
Golden Oak, Polished.
Weight each, 22 pounds.

No. 900.

Fancy Rocker.
Veneer Saddle Seat.
Mahogany Finish, Polished.
Golden Oak, Polished.
Weight each, 20 pounds.

PHOENIX CHAIR CO.
SHEBOYGAN, WIS.

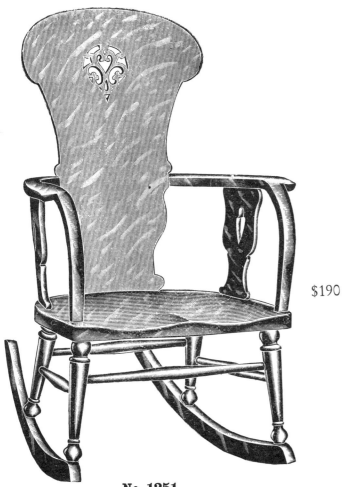

$190

No. 1251.

Fancy Rocker.
Veneer Saddle Seat.
Rodded Arm to Seat.
Mahogany Finish, Polished.
Golden Oak, Polished.
Weight each, 22 pounds.

$180

No. 1252.

Fancy Rocker.
Veneer Saddle Seat.
Early English, Waxed Finish.
Golden Oak, Polished.
Weight each, 24 pounds.

PHOENIX CHAIR CO.
SHEBOYGAN, WIS.

$235

No. 968.

Fancy Rocker.
Veneer Saddle Seat.
Golden Oak, Polished.
Weight each, 20 pounds.

$245

No. 968-D.

Fancy Rocker.
Dark Olive Leather Cobbler Seat.
Golden Oak, Polished.
Weight each, 20 pounds.

PHOENIX CHAIR CO.
SHEBOYGAN, WIS.

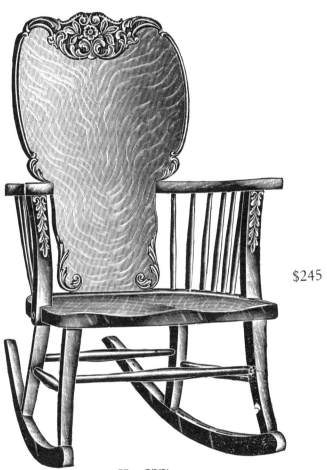

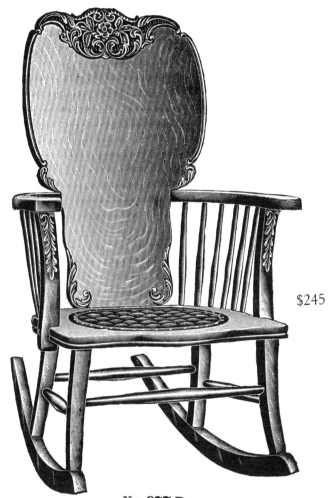

$245

$245

No. 977.

Fancy Rocker.
Veneer Saddle Seat.
Golden Oak, Polished.
Weight each, 23 pounds.

No. 977-D.

Fancy Rocker.
Dark Olive Leather Cobbler Seat.
Golden Oak, Polished.
Weight each, 23 pounds.

PHOENIX CHAIR CO.
SHEBOYGAN, WIS.

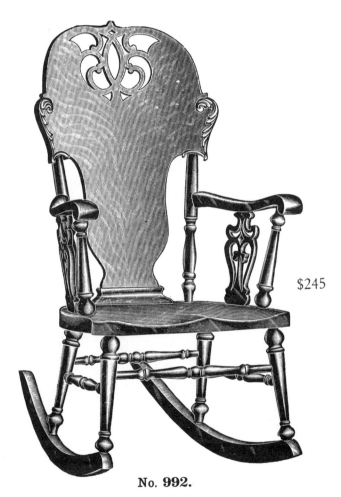

$245

No. 992.

Fancy Rocker.
Veneer Saddle Seat.
Golden Oak, Polished.
Weight each, 21 pounds.

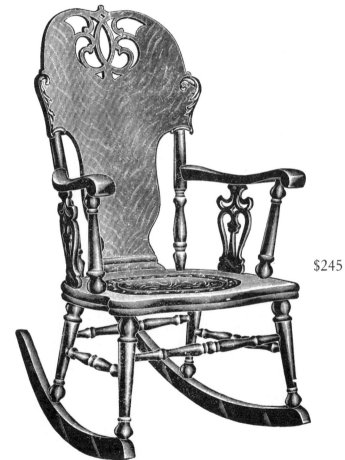

$245

No. 992-D.

Fancy Rocker.
Dark Olive Leather Cobbler Seat.
Golden Oak, Polished.
Weight each, 21 pounds.

PHOENIX CHAIR CO.
SHEBOYGAN, WIS.

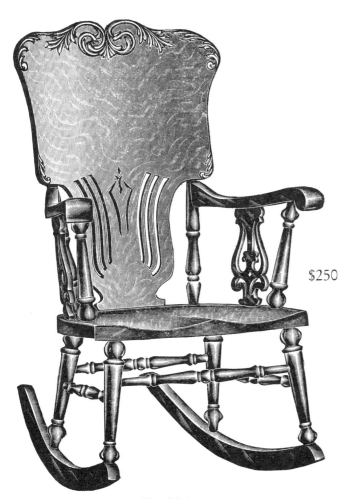

$250

No. 991.

Fancy Rocker.
Veneer Saddle Seat.
Golden Oak, Polished.
Weight each, 22 pounds.

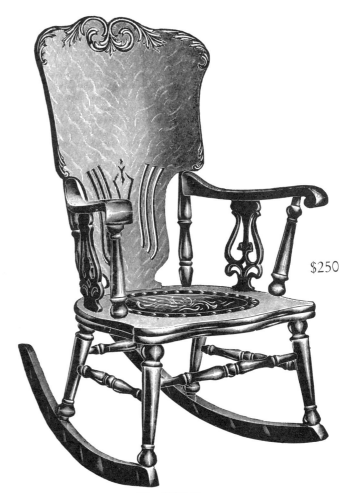

$250

No. 991-D.

Fancy Rocker.
Dark Olive Leather Cobbler Seat.
Golden Oak, Polished.
Weight each, 23 pounds.

PHOENIX CHAIR CO.
SHEBOYGAN, WIS.

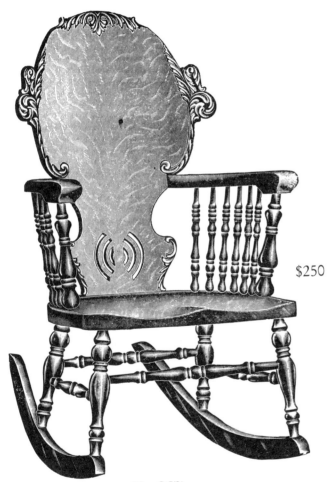

$250

No. 967.

Fancy Rocker.
Veneer Saddle Seat.
Golden Oak, Polished.
Weight each, 21 pounds.

$250

No. 967-D.

Fancy Rocker.
Dark Olive Leather Cobbler Seat.
Golden Oak, Polished.
Weight each, 21 pounds.

PHOENIX CHAIR CO.
SHEBOYGAN, WIS.

$245

No. 196.

Arm Rocker.
Quartered Oak Saddle Wood Seat.
Golden Oak, Polished.
Weight each, 26 pounds.

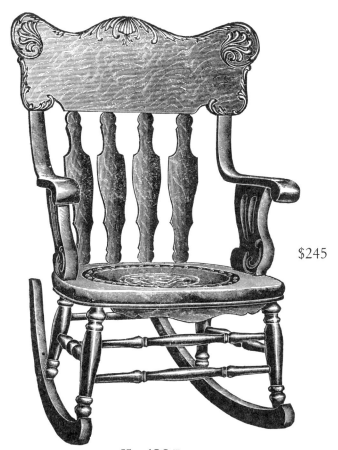

$245

No. 196-D.

Arm Rocker.
Dark Olive Leather Cobbler Seat.
Golden Oak, Polished.
Weight each, 24 pounds.

PHOENIX CHAIR CO.
SHEBOYGAN, WIS.

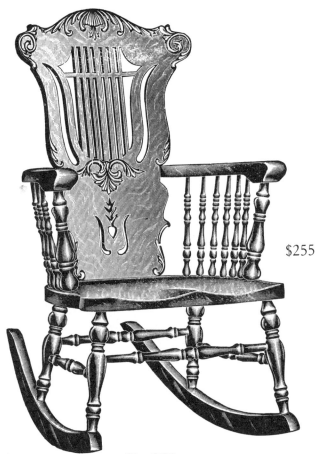

$255

No. 966.

Fancy Rocker.
Veneer Saddle Seat.
Golden Oak, Polished.
Weight each, 20 pounds.

$260

No. 966-D.

Fancy Rocker.
Dark Olive Leather Cobbler Seat.
Golden Oak, Polished.
Weight each, 20 pounds.

PHOENIX CHAIR CO.
SHEBOYGAN, WIS.

$275

No. 704.

Fancy Rocker.
Veneer Roll Seat.
Rodded Arm to Seat.
Golden Oak, Polished.
Weight each, 22 pounds.

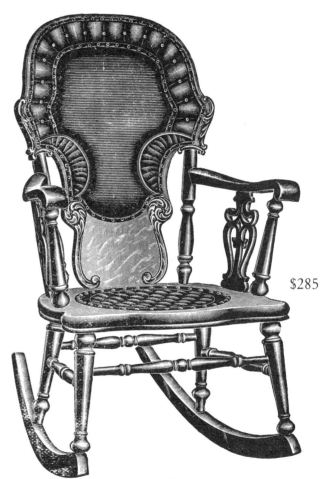

$285

No. 994-DBL.

Fancy Rocker.
Upholstered Dark Olive Leather Back and Cobbler Seat.
Golden Oak, Polished.
Weight each, 26 pounds.

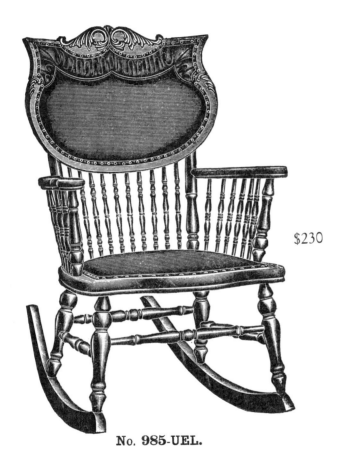

$230

No. 985-UEL.

Fancy Rocker.
Upholstered Dark Olive Leather Seat and Back.
Mahogany Finish, Polished.
Golden Oak, Polished.
Weight each, 22 pounds.

$210

No. 1203-SUBL.

Fancy Rocker.
Upholstered Spanish Leather Back and Spring Seat.
Early English, Waxed Finish.
Golden Oak, Polished.
Weight each, 28 pounds.

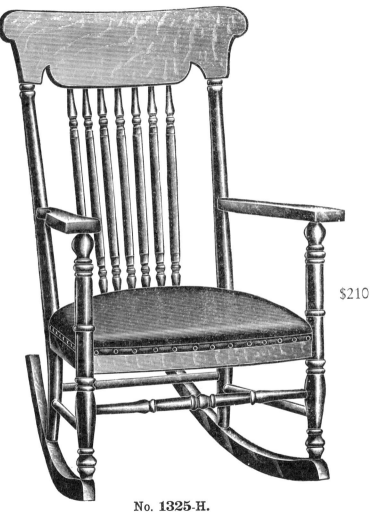

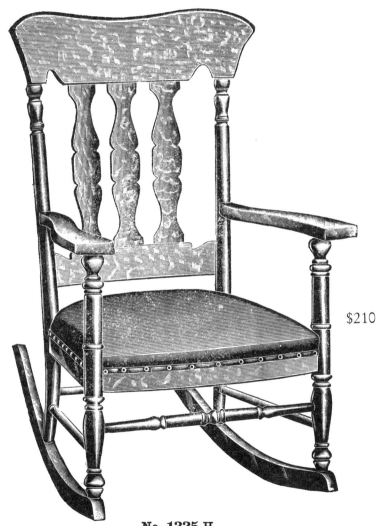

$210

$210

No. 1325-H.

Fancy Rocker.
Upholstered Imitation Leather Spring Seat.
Golden Oak, Gloss.
Weight each, 22 pounds.

No. 1335-H.

Fancy Rocker.
Upholstered Imitation Leather Spring Seat.
Golden Oak, Gloss.
Weight each, 22 pounds.

$220

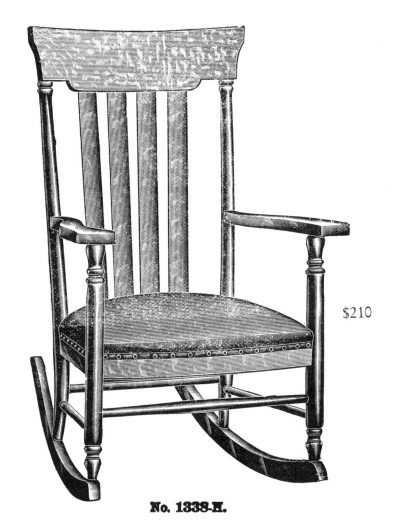

$210

No. 1336-H.

Fancy Rocker.
Upholstered Imitation Leather Spring Seat.
Golden Oak, Gloss.
Weight each, 22 pounds.

No. 1338-H.

Fancy Rocker.
Upholstered Imitation Leather Spring Seat.
Golden Oak, Gloss.
Weight each, 22 pounds.

PHOENIX CHAIR CO.
SHEBOYGAN, WIS.

$220

$225

No. 1339-H.
Fancy Rocker.
Upholstered Imitation Leather Spring Seat.
Golden Oak, Gloss.
Weight each, 23 pounds.

No. 997-H.
Fancy Rocker.
Upholstered Imitation Leather Spring Seat.

No. 997-HL. Same.
Upholstered Genuine Leather Spring Seat.
Golden Oak, Polished.
Weight each, 25 pounds.

PHOENIX CHAIR CO.
SHEBOYGAN, WIS.

$225

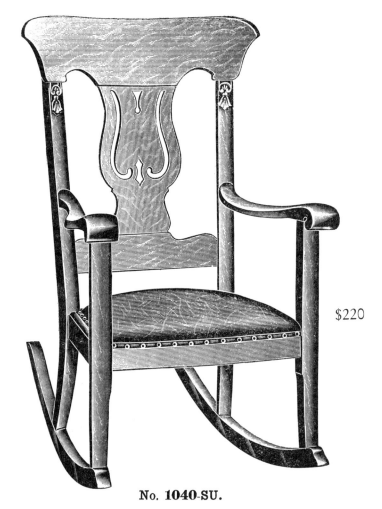

$220

No. 1042-SU.

Fancy Rocker.
Upholstered Imitation Leather Spring Seat.

No. 1042-SUL. Same.

Upholstered Genuine Leather Spring Seat.
Golden Oak, Polished.
Early English, Waxed Finish.
Weight each, 24 pounds.

No. 1040-SU.

Fancy Rocker.
Upholstered Imitation Leather Spring Seat.

No. 1040-SUL. Same.

Upholstered Genuine Leather Spring Seat.
Golden Oak, Polished.
Early English, Waxed Finish.
Weight each, 24 pounds.

PHOENIX CHAIR CO.
SHEBOYGAN, WIS.

$200

$190

No. 1203-SUL.

Fancy Rocker.
Upholstered Spanish Leather Spring Seat.
Early English, Waxed Finish.
Golden Oak, Polished.
Weight each, 25 pounds.

No. 1203-SUBL.

Fancy Rocker.
Upholstered Spanish Leather Back and Spring Seat.
Early English, Waxed Finish.
Golden Oak, Polished.
Weight each, 28 pounds.

PHOENIX CHAIR CO.
SHEBOYGAN, WIS.

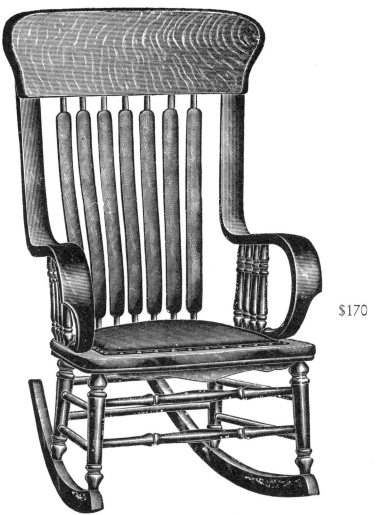

$170

No. 644-SUL.

Large Arm Rocker.
Upholstered Dark Olive Leather Spring Seat.
Rodded Arm to Seat.
Golden Oak, Polished.
Weight each, **28** pounds.

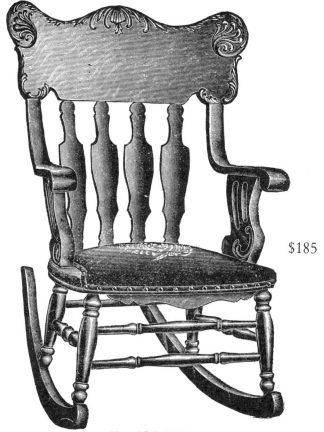

$185

No. 196-SUL.

Arm Rocker.
Upholstered Dark Olive Plain Leather Spring Seat.
Golden Oak, Polished.
Weight each, **27** pounds.

PHOENIX CHAIR CO.
SHEBOYGAN, WIS.

$190

No. 914-HL.

Fancy Rocker
Upholstered Dark Olive Leather Spring Seat.
Golden Oak, Polished.
Weight each, 22 pounds.

$195

No. 941-HL.

Fancy Rocker.
Upholstered Dark Olive Leather Spring Seat.
Golden Oak, Polished.
Weight each, 24 pounds.

PHOENIX CHAIR CO.
SHEBOYGAN WIS.

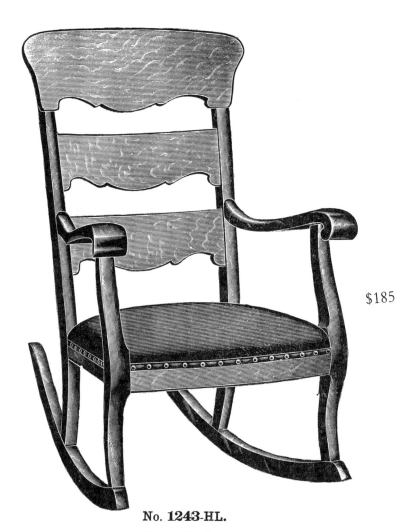

$185

$185

No. 1243-HL.

Fancy Rocker.
Upholstered Dark Olive Leather Spring Seat.
Mahogany Finish, Polished.
Golden Oak, Polished.
Weight each, 22 pounds.

No. 1324-HBL.

Fancy Rocker.
Upholstered Dark Olive Leather Back and Spring Seat.
Golden Oak, Polished.
Weight each, 26 pounds.

PHOENIX CHAIR CO.
SHEBOYGAN, WIS.

$210

No. 941-HBL.

Fancy Rocker.
Upholstered Dark Olive Leather Back and Spring Seat.
Golden Oak, Polished.
Weight each, 25 pounds.

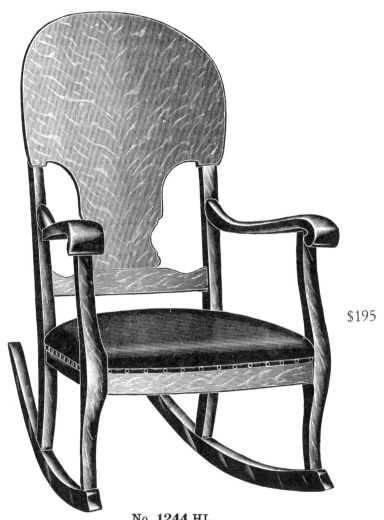

$195

No. 1244-HL.

Fancy Rocker.
Upholstered Dark Olive Leather Spring Seat.
Mahogany Finish, Polished.
Golden Oak, Polished.
Weight each, 22 pounds.

PHOENIX CHAIR CO.
SHEBOYGAN, WIS.

$175

No. 1131-HBL.

Box Seat Arm Chair.
Upholstered Dark Olive Leather Back and **Spring Seat.**
Golden Oak, Polished.
Weight each, 23 pounds.

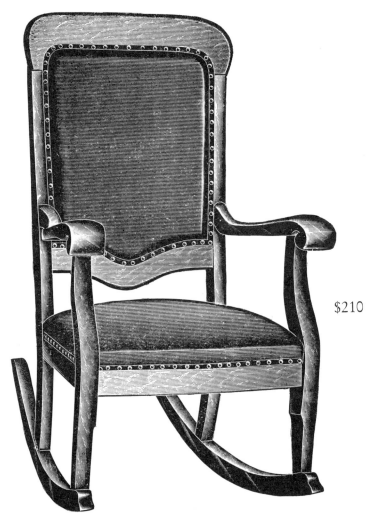

$210

No. 1132-HBL.

Large Arm Rocker.
Upholstered Dark Olive Leather Back and **Spring Seat.**
Mahogany Finish, Polished.
Golden Oak, Polished.
Weight each, 32 pounds.

$320

No. 1134-HBL.

Settee. Length, 40 inches.
Upholstered Dark Olive Leather Back and Spring Seat.
Mahogany Finish, Polished.
Golden Oak, Polished.
Weight each, 40 pounds.

$225

No. 969-HBL.

Fancy Rocker.
Upholstered Dark Olive Leather Back and Spring Seat.
Golden Oak, Polished.
Weight each, 35 pounds.

$210

No. 1250-HBL.

Large Arm Rocker.
Upholstered Dark Olive Leather Spring Seat and Tufted Back.
Golden Oak, Polished.
Weight each, 25 pounds.

PHOENIX CHAIR CO.
SHEBOYGAN, WIS.

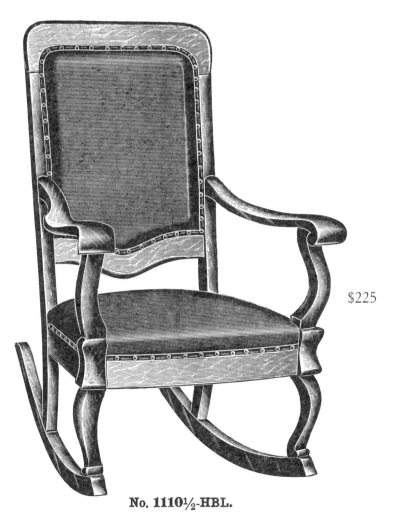

$225

No. 1110½-HBL.
Large Arm Rocker.
Upholstered Dark Olive Leather Back and Spring Seat.
Golden Oak, Polished.
Weight each, 30 pounds.

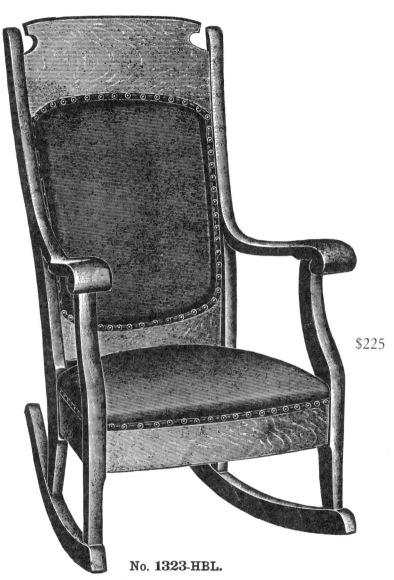

$225

No. 1323-HBL.
Large Arm Rocker.
Upholstered Dark Olive Leather Back and Spring Seat.
Golden Oak, Polished.
Weight each, 36 pounds.

PHOENIX CHAIR CO.
SHEBOYGAN, WIS.

$210

No. 352.

Boston Rocker.
Golden Elm, Gloss.
Weight each, 22 pounds.

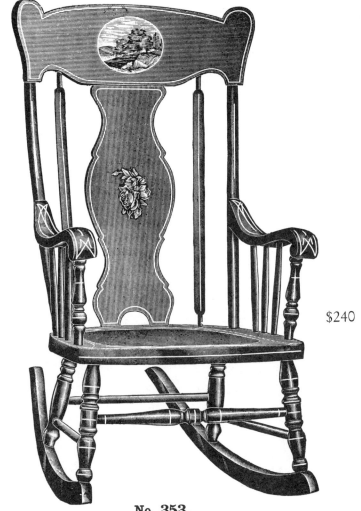

$240

No. 353.

Boston Rocker.
Golden Elm, Gloss.
Weight each, 23 pounds.

PHOENIX CHAIR CO.
SHEBOYGAN, WIS.

$230

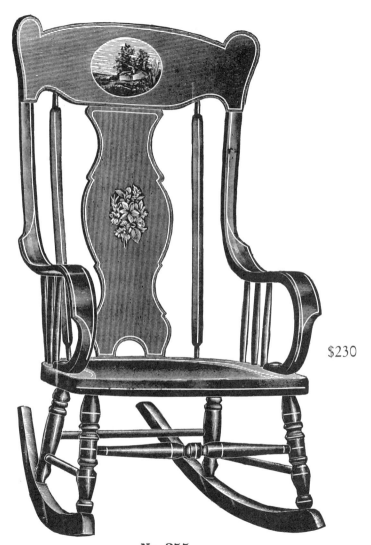

$230

No. 354.

Boston Rocker.
Golden Elm, Gloss.
Weight each, 22 pounds.

No. 355.

Boston Rocker.
Golden Elm, Gloss.
Weight each, 22 pounds.

$250

$240

No. 356.

Boston Rocker.
Golden Elm, Gloss.
Weight each, 23 pounds.

No. 357.

Boston Rocker.
Golden Elm, Gloss.
Weight each, 23 pounds.

PHOENIX CHAIR CO.
SHEBOYGAN, WIS.

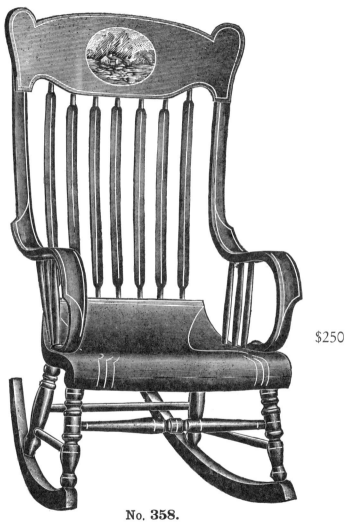

$250

No. 358.

Boston Rocker.
Golden Elm, Gloss.
Weight each, 22 pounds.

$250

No. 360.

Boston Rocker.
Golden Elm, Gloss.
Weight each, 23 pounds.

PHOENIX CHAIR CO.
SHEBOYGAN, WIS.

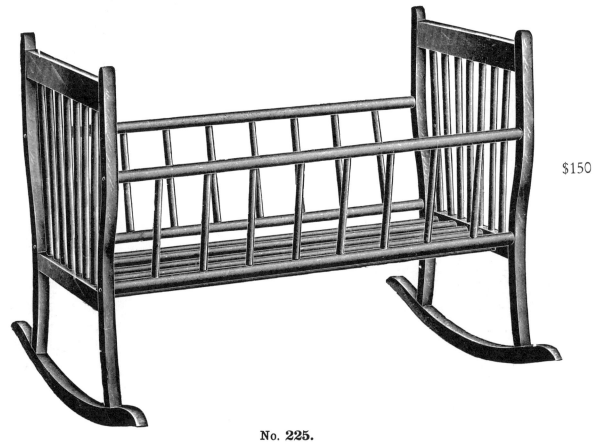

$150

No. 225.

Cradle.
Golden Elm, Gloss.
Weight each, 15 pounds.

PHOENIX CHAIR CO.
SHEBOYGAN, WIS.

$160

No. 221.
Cradle.
Golden Elm, Gloss.
Weight each, 19 pounds.

PHOENIX CHAIR CO.
SHEBOYGAN, WIS.

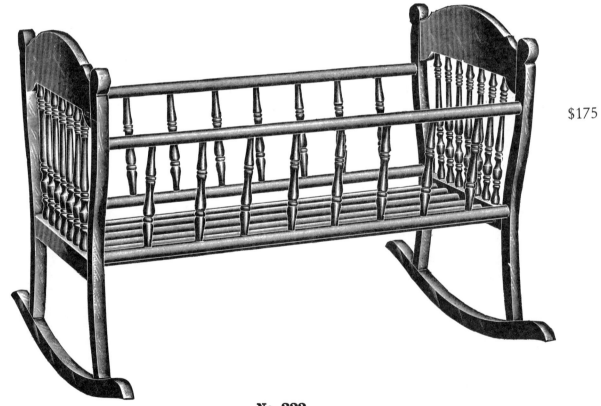

$175

No. 222.

Cradle.
Golden Elm, Gloss.
Weight each, 19 pounds.

PHOENIX CHAIR CO.
SHEBOYGAN, WIS.

$175

No. 223.

Panelled Cradle.
Golden Elm, Gloss.
Weight each, 30 pounds.

PHOENIX CHAIR CO.
SHEBOYGAN, WIS.

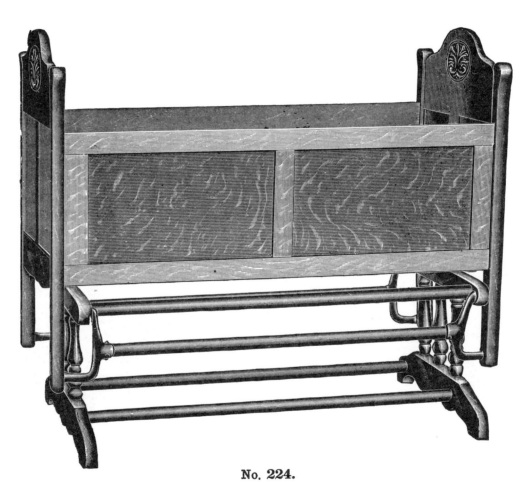

$195

No. 224.

McLean Swing Cradle.
Golden Elm, Gloss.
Weight each, 47 pounds.

$65

$55

$45

No. 242.

Phoenix Walking Chair.
Red or Golden Elm, Gloss.
Weight each, **7** pounds.

PHOENIX CHAIR CO.
SHEBOYGAN WIS.

$100

No. 14.

Child's Chair.
10 in. High.
Red or Golden Elm, Gloss.
Weight each, 4 pounds.

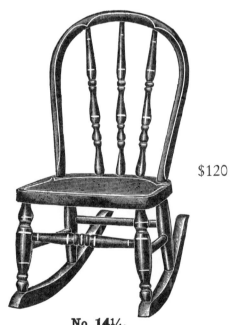

$120

No. 14¼.

Child's Rocker.
Red or Golden Elm, Gloss.
Weight each, 4 pounds.

$100

No. 14½.

Child's Chair.
12 in. High.
Red or Golden Elm, Gloss.
Weight each, 4½ pounds.

PHOENIX CHAIR CO.
SHEBOYGAN, WIS.

$120

No. 14¾.

Child's Rocker.
Red or Golden Elm, Gloss.
Weight each, 4½ pounds.

$100

No. 40½.

Nursery Chair.
Red or Golden Elm, Gloss.
Weight each, 5 pounds.

$110

No. 185½.

Nursery Chair.
Red or Golden Elm, Gloss.
Weight each, 7 pounds.

PHOENIX CHAIR CO.
SHEBOYGAN, WIS.

$95

No. 129.

Kindergarten Chair.
10½ inches High.
Red or Golden Elm, Gloss.
Weight each, 5 pounds.

$95

No. 129½.

Kindergarten Chair.
13½ inches High.
Red or Golden Elm, Gloss.
Weight each, 6 pounds.

PHOENIX CHAIR CO.
SHEBOYGAN, WIS.

$100

No. 132.

Kindergarten Rocker.
Red or Golden Elm, Gloss.
Weight each, 6 pounds.

$110

No. 117½.

Child's Rocker.
Red or Golden Elm, Gloss.
Weight each, 7 pounds.

$120

No. 117½-PB.

Child's Rocker.
Wood Seat.
Perforated Veneer Back.
Red or Golden Elm, Gloss.
Weight each, 7 pounds.

PHOENIX CHAIR CO.
SHEBOYGAN, WIS.

$110

$120

No. 98½.

Child's High Chair.
Wood Seat.
Red or Golden Elm, Gloss.
Weight each, 9 pounds.

No. 89½-S.

Child's High Chair.
Red or Golden Elm, Gloss.
Weight each, 11 pounds.

PHOENIX CHAIR CO.

$135

$145

No. 635-S.

Child's High Chair.
Wood Seat.
Golden Elm, Gloss.
Weight each, 12 pounds.

No. 637.

Child's Rocker.
Wood Seat.
Golden Elm, Gloss.
Weight each, 8 pounds.

PHOENIX CHAIR CO.
SHEBOYGAN, WIS.

$145

$155

No. 636-S.

Child's High Chair.
Cane Seat.
Golden Elm, Gloss.
Weight each, 11 pounds.

No. 638.

Child's Rocker.
Cane Seat.
Golden Elm, Gloss.
Weight each, 8 pounds.

PHOENIX CHAIR CO.
SHEBOYGAN, WIS.

$145

$145

No. 627-S.

Child's High Chair.
Wood Seat.
Golden Elm, Gloss.
Weight each, 12 pounds.

No. 627½.

Child's Rocker.
Wood Seat.
Golden Elm, Gloss.
Weight each, 9 pounds.

PHOENIX CHAIR CO.
SHEBOYGAN, WIS.

$175

No. 631.

Child's High Chair.
Wood Seat.
Golden Elm, Gloss.
Weight each, 12 pounds.

$165

No. 633.

Child's Rocker.
Wood Seat.
Golden Elm, Gloss.
Weight each, 8 pounds.

$145

No. 617-S.

Child's High Chair.
Wood Seat.
Golden Elm, Gloss.
Weight each, 13 pounds.

$145

No. 619.

Child's Rocker.
Wood Seat.
Golden Elm, Gloss.
Weight each, 8 pounds.

PHOENIX CHAIR CO.
SHEBOYGAN, WIS.

$155

No. 618-S.

Child's High Chair.
Cane Seat.
Golden Elm, Gloss.
Weight each, 12 pounds.

$155

No. 620.

Child's Rocker.
Cane Seat.
Golden Elm, Gloss.
Weight each, 7 pounds.

PHOENIX CHAIR CO.
SHEBOYGAN, WIS.

$165

$165

No. 731-S.

Child's High Chair.
Wood Seat.
Golden Elm, Gloss.
Weight each, 10 pounds.

No. 733.

Child's Rocker.
Wood Seat.
Golden Elm, Gloss.
Weight each, 6 pounds:

PHOENIX CHAIR CO.
SHEBOYGAN, WIS.

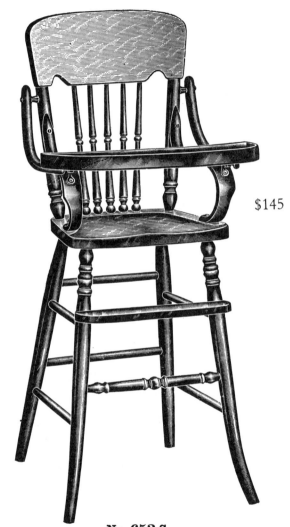

$145

$150

No. 653-S.

Child's High Chair.
Wood Seat.
Golden Elm, Gloss.
Weight each, 12 pounds.

No. 653½.

Child's Rocker.
Wood Seat.
Golden Elm, Gloss.
Weight each, 9 pounds.

$135

$140

No. 651-S.

Child's High Chair.
Wood Seat.
Golden Elm, Gloss.
Weight each, 12 pounds.

No. 651½.

Child's Rocker.
Wood Seat.
Golden Elm, Gloss.
Weight each, 9 pounds.

PHOENIX CHAIR CO.
SHEBOYGAN, WIS.

$145

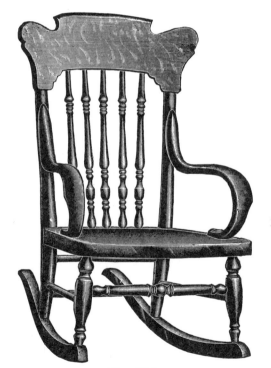

$150

No. 609.

Child's High Chair.
Quartered Oak Wood Seat.
Golden Oak, Gloss.
Weight each, 11 pounds.

No. 611.

Child's Rocker.
Quartered Oak Wood Seat.
Golden Oak, Gloss.
Weight each, 9 pounds.

PHOENIX CHAIR CO.
SHEBOYGAN, WIS.

$155

No. 610.

Child's High Chair.
Cane Seat.
Golden Oak, Gloss.
Weight each, 10 pounds.

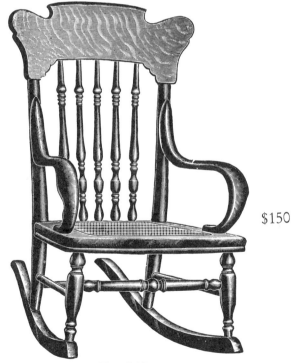

$150

No. 612.

Child's Rocker.
Cane Seat.
Golden Oak, Gloss.
Weight each, 8 pounds.

PHOENIX CHAIR CO.
SHEBOYGAN, WIS.

$145

$150

No. 77.

Child's High Chair.
Wood Seat.
Golden Oak, Gloss.
Weight each, 13 pounds.

No. 79.

Child's Rocker.
Wood Seat.
Golden Oak, Gloss.
Weight each, 9 pounds.

PHOENIX CHAIR CO.
SHEBOYGAN, WIS.

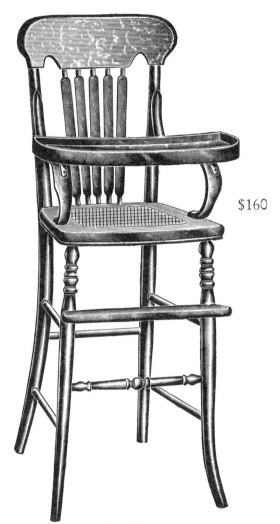

$160

$160

No. 78.
Child's High Chair.
Cane Seat.
Golden Oak, Gloss.
Weight each, 12 pounds.

No. 80.
Child's Rocker.
Cane Seat.
Golden Oak, Gloss.
Weight each, 8 pounds.

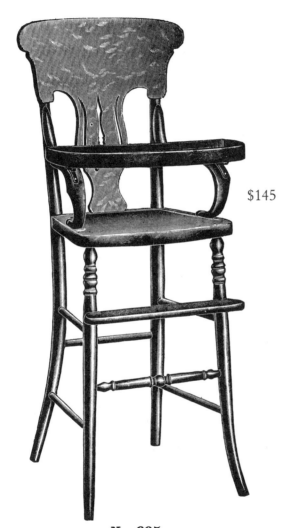

$145

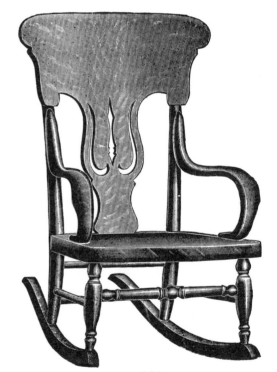

$150

No. 605.

Child's High Chair.
Quartered Oak Wood Seat.
Golden Oak, Polished.
Weight each, 15 pounds.

No. 607.

Child's Rocker.
Quartered Oak Wood Seat.
Golden Oak, Polished.
Weight each, 10 pounds.

PHOENIX CHAIR CO.
SHEBOYGAN, WIS.

$160

No. 606.

Child's High Chair.
Cane Seat.
Golden Oak, Polished.
Weight each, 14 pounds.

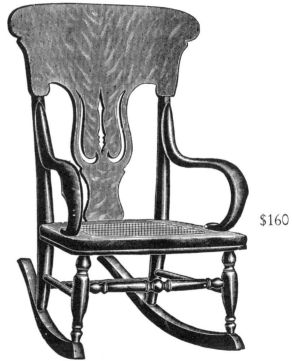

$160

No. 608.

Child's Rocker.
Cane Seat.
Golden Oak, Polished.
Weight each, 10 pounds.

$150

No. 538½-S.

Child's Vienna High Chair.
Quartered Oak Wood Seat.
Cane Back.
Golden Oak, Gloss.
Weight each, 12 pounds.

$150

No. 538-S.

Child's Vienna High Chair.
Cane Seat and Back.
Golden Oak, Gloss.
Weight each, 10 pounds.

PHOENIX CHAIR CO.
SHEBOYGAN, WIS.

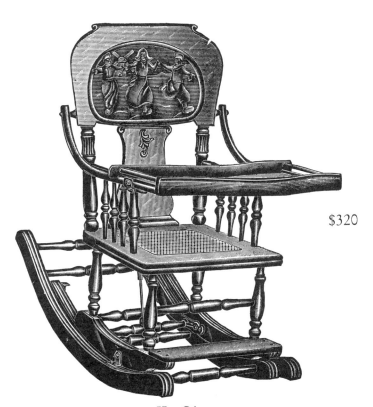

$320

No. 81.

Child's Combination High and Rocking Chair.
High Chair, 24 inches.
Rocker, 14 inches. } Floor to Seat.
Golden Oak Finish, Gloss.
Weight each, 20 pounds.

$320

No. 82.

Child's Combination High and Wheel Chair.
Without Push Handle.
High Chair, 24 inches.
Youth's Chair, 21 inches. } Floor to Seat.
Wheel Chair, 15 inches.
Golden Oak Finish, Gloss.
Weight each, 20 pounds.

PHOENIX CHAIR CO.
SHEBOYGAN, WIS.

$340

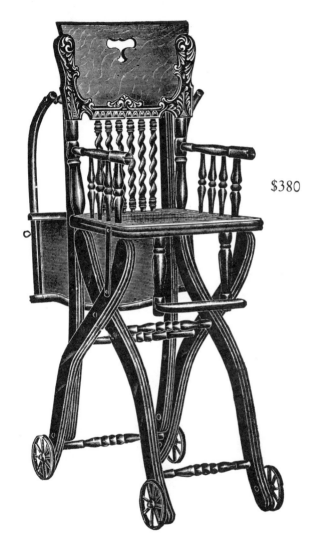

$380

No. 84.

Child's Combination High and Wheel Chair.
With Push Handle.
High Chair, 24 inches. ⎫
Wheel Chair, 14 inches. ⎬ Floor to Seat.
Golden Oak Finish, Gloss.
Weight each, 20 pounds.

PHOENIX CHAIR CO.
SHEBOYGAN, WIS.

$365

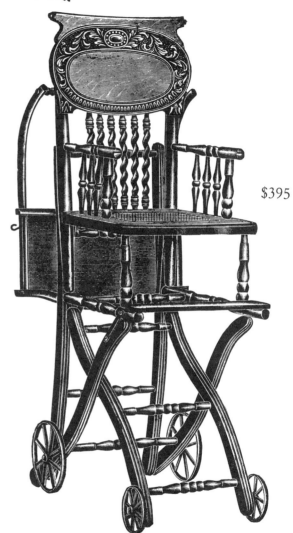

$395

No. 83.

Child's Combination High and Wheel Chair.
With Push Handle.
High Chair, 24 inches. } Floor to Seat.
Wheel Chair, 14 inches. }
Golden Oak Finish, Gloss.
Weight each, 20 pounds.

PHOENIX CHAIR CO.
SHEBOYGAN, WIS.

$160

$190

No. 99.
Youth's High Chair.
Wood Seat.
Golden Elm, Gloss.
Weight each, 11 pounds.

No. 101.
Misses' Rocker.
Wood Seat.
Golden Elm, Gloss.
Weight each, 14 pounds.

$160

No. 100.

Youth's High Chair.
Cane Seat.
Golden Elm, Gloss.
Weight each, 9 pounds.

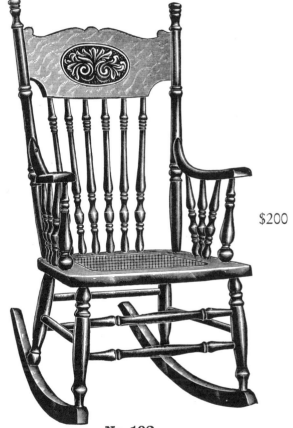

$200

No. 102.

Misses' Rocker.
Cane Seat.
Golden Elm, Gloss.
Weight each, 12 pounds.

PHOENIX CHAIR CO.
SHEBOYGAN, WIS.

$170

$210

No. 41.

Youth's High Chair.
Wood Seat.
Golden Elm, Gloss.
Weight each, 11 pounds.

No. 43.

Misses' Rocker.
Wood Seat.
Golden Elm, Gloss.
Weight each, 14 pounds.

PHOENIX CHAIR CO.
SHEBOYGAN, WIS.

$180

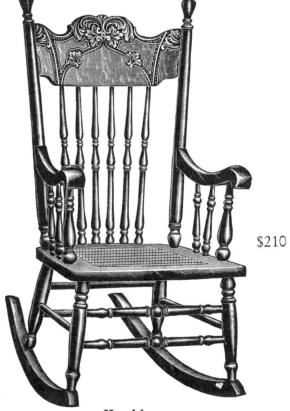

$210

No. 42.
Youth's High Chair.
Cane Seat.
Golden Elm, Gloss.
Weight each, 9 pounds.

No. 44.
Misses' Rocker.
Cane Seat.
Golden Elm, Gloss.
Weight each, 12 pounds.

PHOENIX CHAIR CO.
SHEBOYGAN, WIS.

$145

$170

No. 91.

Youth's High Chair.
Veneer Seat.
Golden Oak, Gloss.
Weight each, 12 pounds.

No. 93.

Misses' Rocker.
Veneer Seat.
Golden Oak, Gloss.
Weight each, 13 pounds.

PHOENIX CHAIR CO.
SHEBOYGAN, WIS.

$95

$105

No. 592½.

Ladies' Dressing Chair.
22 inches High.
Veneer Seat.
Golden Oak, Polished.
Weight each, 9 pounds.

No. 592.

Ladies' Dressing Chair.
22 inches High.
Cane Seat.
Golden Oak, Polished.
Weight each, 9 pounds.

$250

$250

No. 107.

Misses' Rocker.
Wood Seat.
Golden Elm, Gloss.
Weight each, 14 pounds.

No. 108.

Misses' Rocker.
Cane Seat.
Golden Elm, Gloss.
Weight each, 13 pounds.

$250

No. 988-D.

Misses' Rocker.
Dark Olive Leather Cobbler Seat.
Golden Elm, Gloss.
Weight each, 14 pounds.

$250

No. 986-D.

Misses' Rocker.
Dark Olive Leather Cobbler Seat.
Golden Elm, Gloss.
Weight each, 14 pounds.

PHOENIX CHAIR CO.
SHEBOYGAN, WIS.

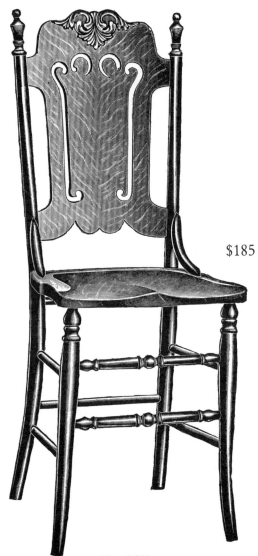

$185

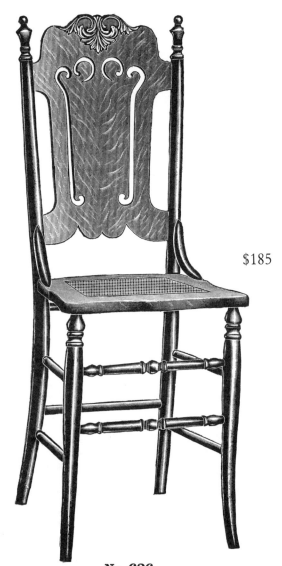

$185

No. 625.

Youth's High Chair.
Quartered Saddle Wood Seat.
Golden Oak, Polished.
Weight each, 12 pounds.

No. 626.

Youth's High Chair.
Cane Seat.
Golden Oak, Polished.
Weight each, 11 pounds.

PHOENIX CHAIR CO.
SHEBOYGAN, WIS.

$160

No. 574½.

Youth's High Chair.
Veneer Seat.
Golden Oak, Polished.
Weight each, 10 pounds.

$175

No. 574.

Youth's High Chair.
Cane Seat.
Golden Oak, Polished.
Weight each, 9 pounds.

$170

$180

No. 524½.

Youth's High Chair.
Veneer Seat.
Golden Oak, Polished.
Weight each, 10 pounds.

No. 524.

Youth's High Chair.
Cane Seat.
Golden Oak, Polished.
Weight each, 10 pounds.

PHOENIX CHAIR CO.
SHEBOYGAN, WIS.

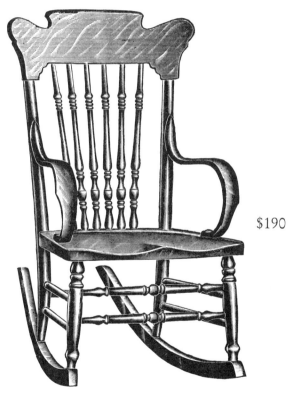

$190

No. 611½.

Misses' Rocker.
Veneer Saddle Seat.
Golden Oak, Polished.
Weight each, 14 pounds.

$185

No. 607½.

Misses' Rocker.
Veneer Saddle Seat.
Golden Oak, Polished.
Weight each, 14 pounds.

PHOENIX CHAIR CO.
SHEBOYGAN, WIS.

$165

$175

No. 34.

Arm Chair.
Wood Seat.
Rodded Arm to Seat.
Golden Elm, Gloss.
Weight each, 15 pounds.

No. 33.

Arm Chair.
Cane Seat.
Rodded Arm to Seat.
Golden Elm, Gloss.
Weight each, 11 pounds.

PHOENIX CHAIR CO.
SHEBOYGAN, WIS.

$180

No. 30.

Arm Chair.
Wood Seat.
Rodded Arm to Seat.
Golden Elm, Gloss.
Weight each, 15 pounds.

$180

No. 29.

Arm Chair.
Cane Seat.
Rodded Arm to Seat.
Golden Elm, Gloss.
Weight each, 11 pounds.

PHOENIX CHAIR CO.
SHEBOYGAN, WIS.

$185

$210

No. 13.

Arm Chair.
Cane Seat and Back.
Rodded Arm to Seat.
Golden Elm, Gloss.
Weight each, 12 pounds.

No. 1.

Office Chair.
Adjustable, Revolving and Tilting.
Cane Seat and Back.
Rodded Arm to Seat.
Golden Oak, Gloss.
Weight each, 31 pounds.

PHOENIX CHAIR CO.
SHEBOYGAN, WIS.

$190

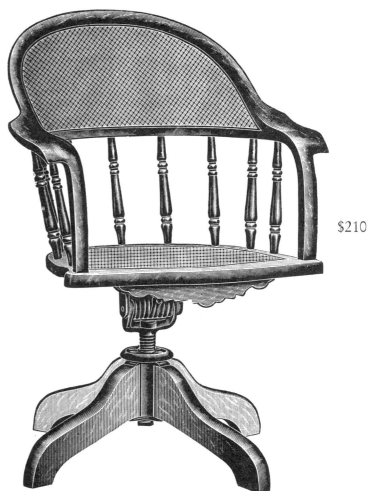

$210

No. 13½.

Arm Chair.
Cane Seat and Back.
Wide Arms.
Rodded Arm to Seat.
Golden Elm, Gloss.
Weight each, 13 pounds.

No. 1¼.

Office Chair.
Adjustable, Revolving and Tilting.
Cane Seat and Back.
Rodded Arm to Seat.
Golden Oak, Gloss.
Weight each, 31 pounds.

PHOENIX CHAIR CO.
SHEBOYGAN, WIS.

$275

No. 2.

Office Chair.

Adjustable, Revolving and Tilting.   Cane Seat and Back,
Rodded Arm to Seat.   Golden Oak, Polished,
Weight each, 33 pounds.

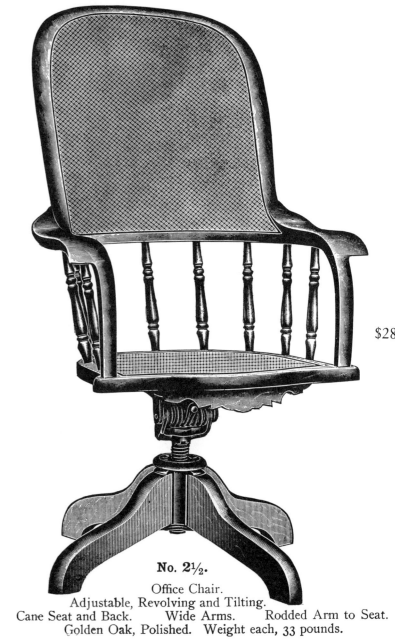

$285

No. 2½.

Office Chair.

Adjustable, Revolving and Tilting.
Cane Seat and Back.   Wide Arms.   Rodded Arm to Seat.
Golden Oak, Polished.   Weight each, 33 pounds.

PHOENIX CHAIR CO.
SHEBOYGAN, WIS.

$180

No. 419.

Arm Chair.
Wood Seat.
Golden Elm, Gloss.
Weight each, 18 pounds.

$180

No. 417.

Arm Chair.
Wood Seat.
Golden Elm, Gloss.
Weight each, 18 pounds.

PHOENIX CHAIR CO.
SHEBOYGAN, WIS.

$180

No. 383.

Arm Chair.
Wood Seat.
Golden Elm, Gloss.
Weight each, 17 pounds.

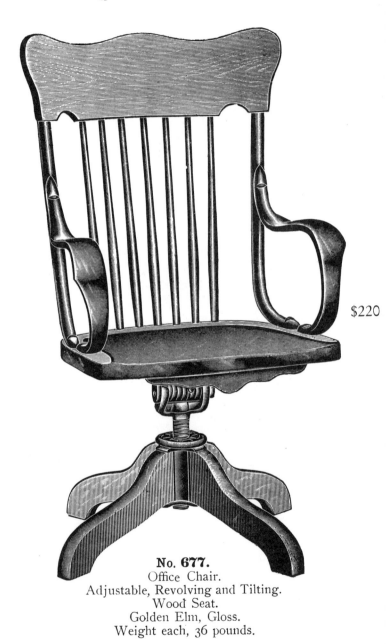

$220

No. 677.

Office Chair.
Adjustable, Revolving and Tilting.
Wood Seat.
Golden Elm, Gloss.
Weight each, 36 pounds.

PHOENIX CHAIR CO.
SHEBOYGAN, WIS.

$180

No. 384.

Arm Chair.   Cane Seat.
Golden Elm, Gloss.   Weight each, 14 pounds.

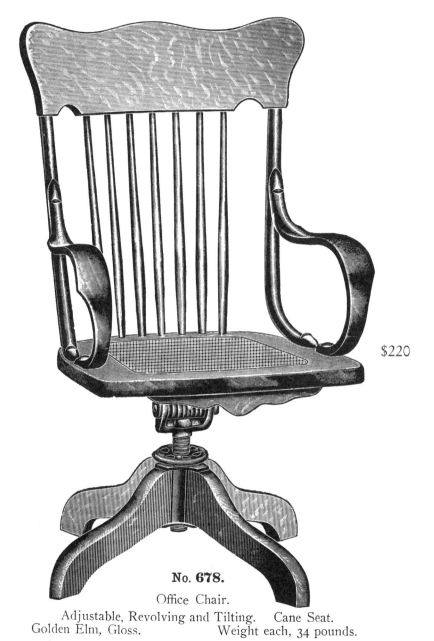

$220

No. 678.

Office Chair.
Adjustable, Revolving and Tilting.   Cane Seat.
Golden Elm, Gloss.   Weight each, 34 pounds.

PHOENIX CHAIR CO.
SHEBOYGAN, WIS.

$180

$220

No. 363.

Arm Chair.
Wood Seat.
Golden Elm, Gloss.
Weight each, 19 pounds.

No. 371.

Office Chair.
Adjustable, Revolving and Tilting.
Wood Seat.
Golden Elm, Gloss.
Weight each, 36 pounds.

PHOENIX CHAIR CO.
SHEBOYGAN, WIS.

$200

No. 364.

Arm Chair.
Cane Seat.
Golden Elm, Gloss.
Weight each, 15 pounds.

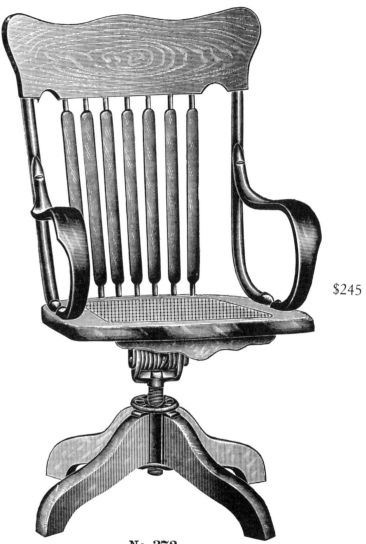

$245

No. 372.

Office Chair.
Adjustable, Revolving and Tilting.
Cane Seat.
Golden Elm, Gloss.
Weight each, 34 pounds.

PHOENIX CHAIR CO.
SHEBOYGAN, WIS.

$220

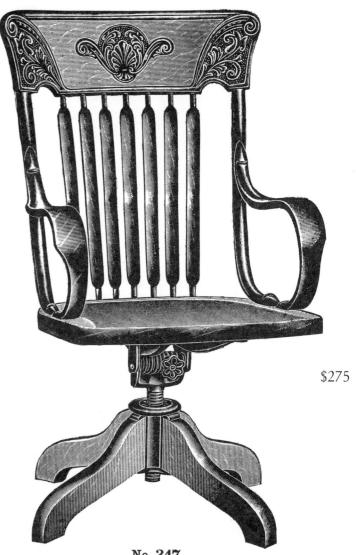

$275

No. 343.

Arm Chair.
Wood Seat.
Golden Elm, Gloss.
Weight each, 18 pounds.

No. 347.

Office Chair.
Adjustable, Revolving and Tilting.
Wood Seat.
Golden Elm, Gloss.
Weight each, 36 pounds.

PHOENIX CHAIR CO.
SHEBOYGAN, WIS.

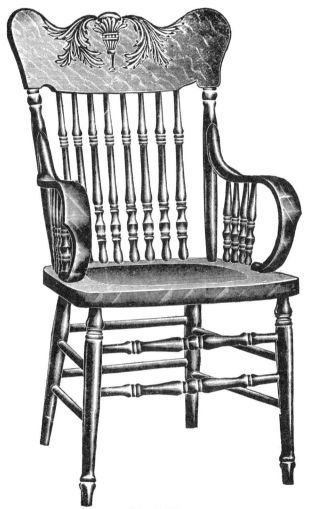

$2 50

$2 50

No. 305.

Arm Chair.
Wood Seat.
Golden Elm, Gloss.
Weight each, 21 pounds.

No. 306.

Arm Chair.
Cane Seat.
Golden Elm, Gloss.
Weight each, 18 pounds.

PHOENIX CHAIR CO.
SHEBOYGAN, WIS.

$250

No. 263.

Arm Chair.
Wood Seat.
Golden Elm, Gloss.
Weight each, 19 pounds.

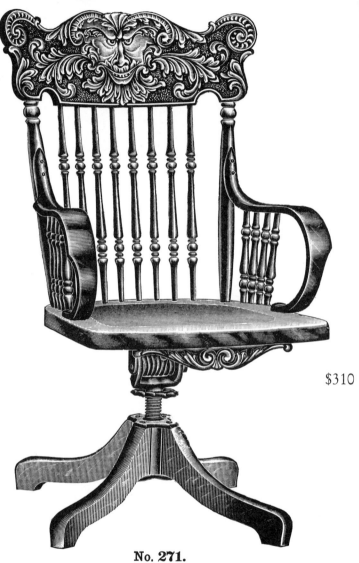

$310

No. 271.

Office Chair.
Adjustable, Revolving and Tilting.
Wood Seat.
Golden Elm, Gloss.
Weight each, 37 pounds.

PHOENIX CHAIR CO.
SHEBOYGAN, WIS.

$275

No. 264.

Arm Chair.
Cane Seat.
Golden Elm, Gloss.
Weight each, 17 pounds.

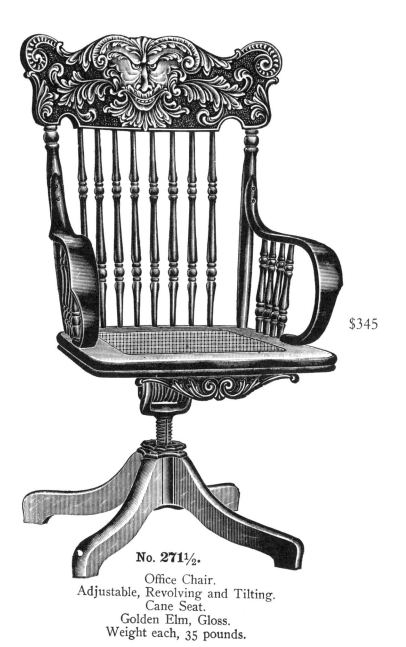

$345

No. 271½.

Office Chair.
Adjustable, Revolving and Tilting.
Cane Seat.
Golden Elm, Gloss.
Weight each, 35 pounds.

PHOENIX CHAIR CO.
SHEBOYGAN, WIS.

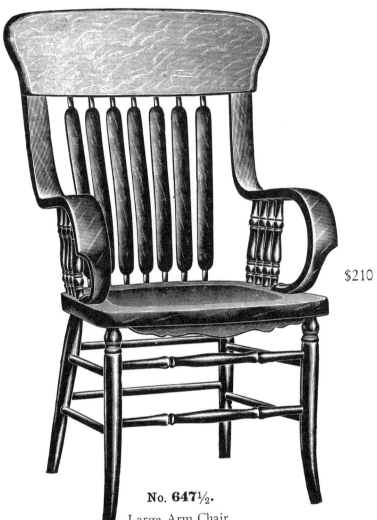

$210

No. 647½.

Large Arm Chair.
Wood Seat.
Rodded Arm to Seat.
Golden Elm, Gloss.
Weight each, **23 pounds.**

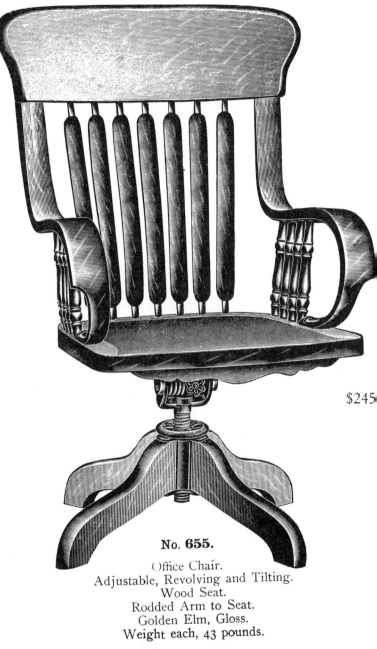

$245

No. 655.

Office Chair.
Adjustable, Revolving and Tilting.
Wood Seat.
Rodded Arm to Seat.
Golden Elm, Gloss.
Weight each, **43 pounds.**

PHOENIX CHAIR CO.
SHEBOYGAN, WIS.

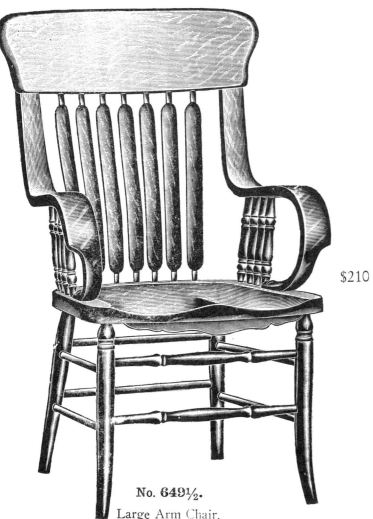

$210

No. 649½.

Large Arm Chair.

Saddle Wood Seat. Rodded Arm to Seat.
Golden Elm, Gloss. Weight each, 23 pounds.

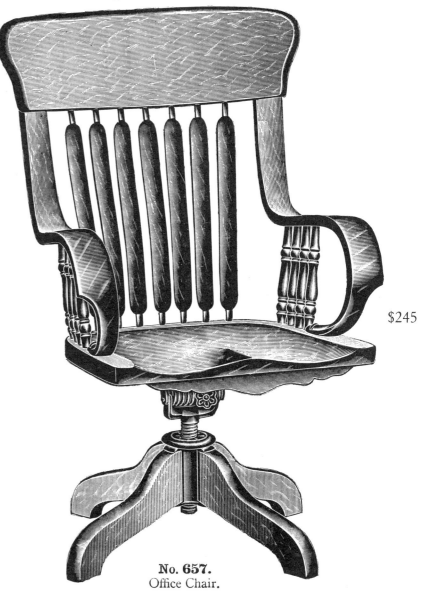

$245

No. 657.

Office Chair.

Adjustable, Revolving and Tilting.
Saddle Wood Seat. Rodded Arm to Seat.
Golden Elm, Gloss. Weight each, 43 pounds.

$285

$345

No. 387½.

Arm Chair.

Wood Seat.   Rodded Arm to Seat.

Golden Elm, Gloss.   Weight each, 23 pounds.

No. 391½.

Office Chair.

Adjustable, Revolving and Tilting.   Wood Seat.

Rodded Arm to Seat.   Golden Elm, Gloss.   Weight each, 40 pounds.

PHOENIX CHAIR CO.
SHEBOYGAN, WIS.

$285

No. 387.
Arm Chair.
Saddle Wood Seat. Rodded Arm to Seat. Golden Elm, Gloss.
Weight each, 23 pounds.

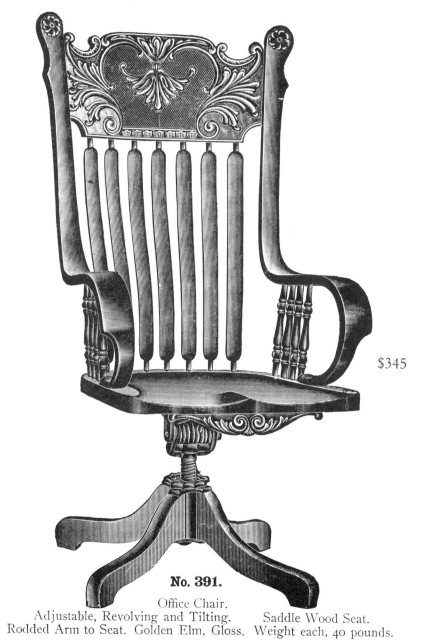

$345

No. 391.
Office Chair.
Adjustable, Revolving and Tilting. Saddle Wood Seat.
Rodded Arm to Seat. Golden Elm, Gloss. Weight each, 40 pounds.

PHOENIX CHAIR CO.
SHEBOYGAN, WIS.

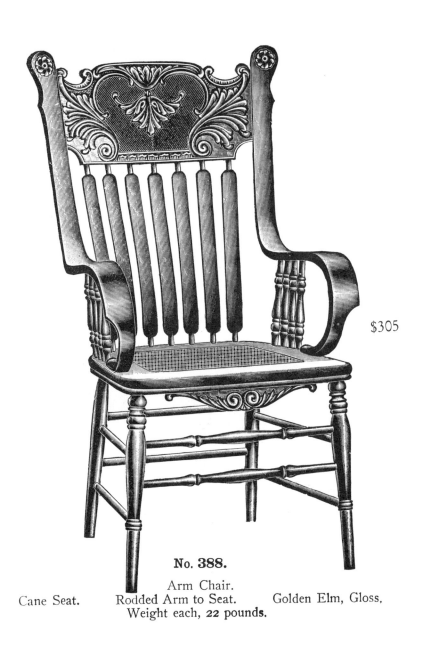

$305

No. 388.

Arm Chair.

Cane Seat.   Rodded Arm to Seat.   Golden Elm, Gloss.
Weight each, **22 pounds.**

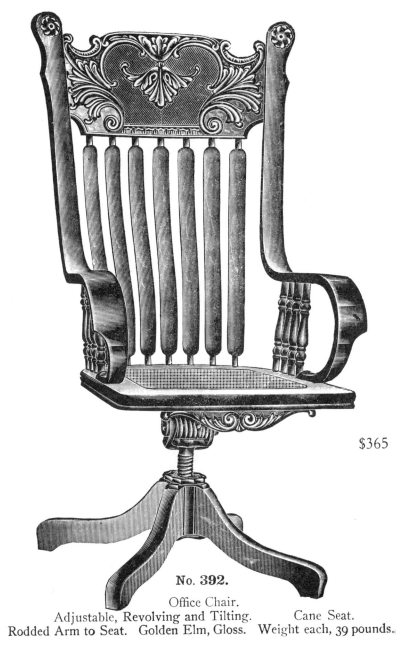

$365

No. 392.

Office Chair.
Adjustable, Revolving and Tilting.   Cane Seat.
Rodded Arm to Seat.   Golden Elm, Gloss.   Weight each, 39 pounds.

PHOENIX CHAIR CO.
SHEBOYGAN, WIS.

$295

No. 388-D.
Large Arm Chair.
Dark Olive Leather Cobbler Seat. Rodded Arm to Seat.
Golden Elm, Gloss. Weight each, 22 pounds.

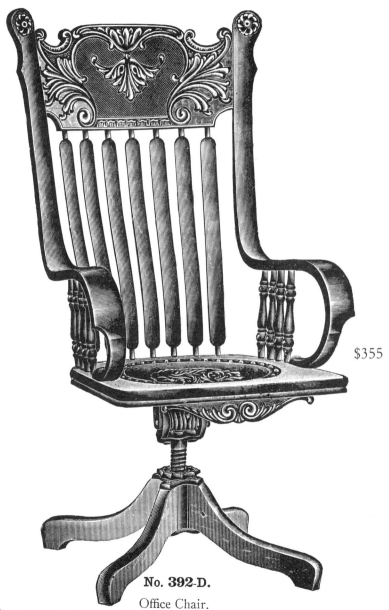

$355

No. 392-D.
Office Chair.
Adjustable, Revolving and Tilting. Dark Olive Leather Cobbler Seat.
Rodded Arm to Seat. Golden Elm, Gloss. Weight each, 39 pounds.

PHOENIX CHAIR CO.
SHEBOYGAN, WIS.

$290

No. 231.
Arm Chair.
Wood Seat.   Rodded Arm to Seat.   Golden Elm, Gloss.
Weight each, 23 pounds.

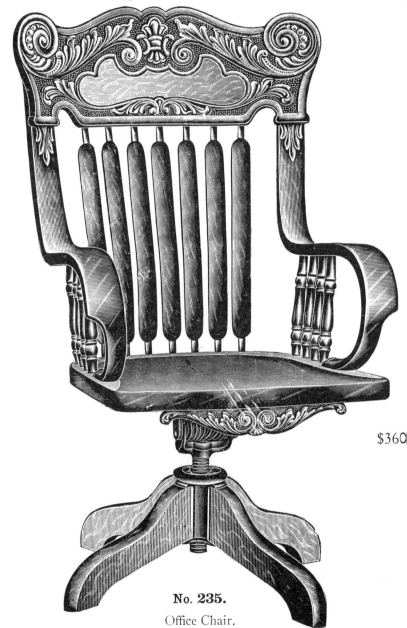

$360

No. 235.
Office Chair.
Adjustable, Revolving and Tilting.   Wood Seat.
Rodded Arm to Seat. Golden Elm, Gloss. Weight each, 43 pounds.

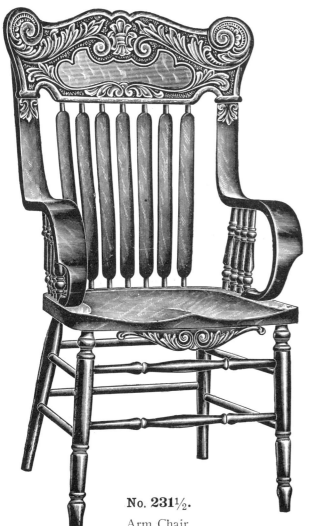

$290

No. 231½.
Arm Chair.
Saddle Wood Seat.
Rodded Arm to Seat.
Golden Elm, Gloss.
Weight each, 23 pounds.

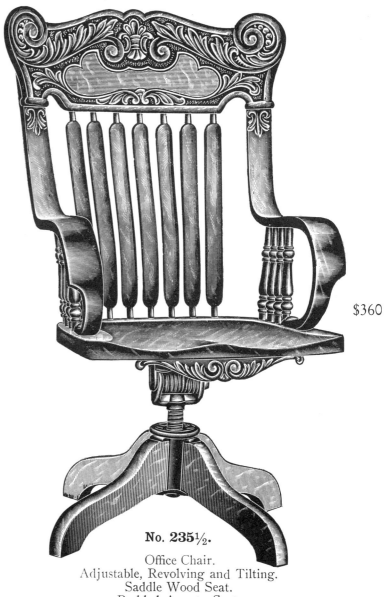

$360

No. 235½.
Office Chair.
Adjustable, Revolving and Tilting.
Saddle Wood Seat.
Rodded Arm to Seat.
Golden Elm, Gloss.
Weight each, 43 pounds.

PHOENIX CHAIR CO.
SHEBOYGAN, WIS.

$310

$375

No. 232.

Arm Chair.
Cane Seat.
Rodded Arm to Seat.
Golden Elm, Gloss.
Weight each, 24 pounds.

No. 236.

Office Chair.
Adjustable, Revolving and Tilting.
Cane Seat.
Rodded Arm to Seat.
Golden Elm, Gloss.
Weight each, 40 pounds.

PHOENIX CHAIR CO.
SHEBOYGAN, WIS.

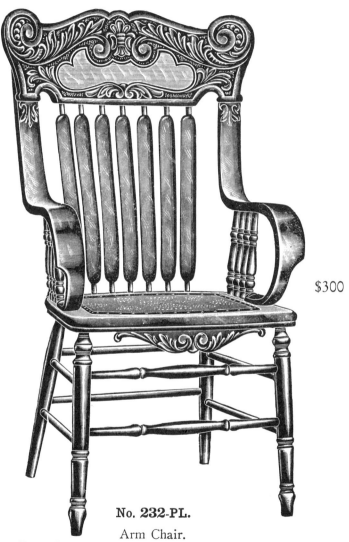

$300

No. 232-PL.

Arm Chair.
Dark Olive Perforated Leather Seat over Cane
Rodded Arm to Seat.
Golden Elm, Gloss.
Weight each, 24 pounds.

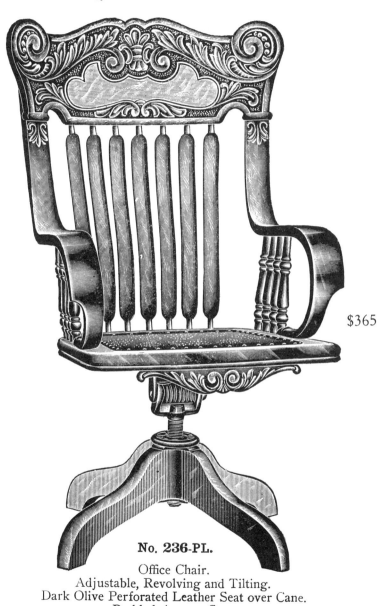

$365

No. 236-PL.

Office Chair.
Adjustable, Revolving and Tilting.
Dark Olive Perforated Leather Seat over Cane.
Rodded Arm to Seat.
Golden Elm, Gloss.
Weight each, 40 pounds.

PHOENIX CHAIR CO.
SHEBOYGAN, WIS.

$170

No. 519¼.

Arm Chair.
Veneer Seat.
Golden Oak, Polished.
Weight each, 12 pounds.

$220

No. 519¾.

Office Chair.
Adjustable, Revolving and Tilting.
Veneer Seat.
Golden Oak, Polished.
Weight each, 22 pounds.

PHOENIX CHAIR CO.
SHEBOYGAN, WIS.

$180

$230

No. 520¼.

Arm Chair.
Cane Seat.
Golden Oak, Polished.
Weight each, 12 pounds.

No. 520¾.

Office Chair.
Adjustable, Revolving and Tilting.
Cane Seat.
Golden Oak, Polished.
Weight each, 22 pounds.

PHOENIX CHAIR CO.
SHEBOYGAN, WIS.

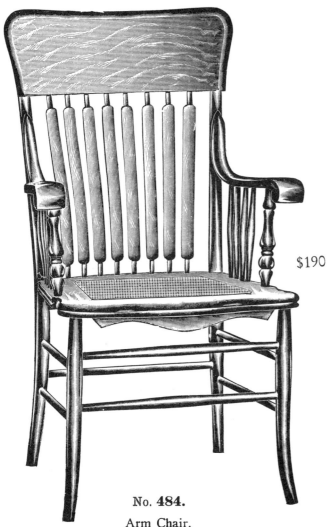

$190

No. 484.

Arm Chair.
Cane Seat.
Golden Oak, Polished.
Weight each, 18 pounds.

$245

No. 492.

Office Chair.
Adjustable, Revolving and Tilting.
Cane Seat.
Golden Oak, Polished.
Weight each, 39 pounds.

PHOENIX CHAIR CO.
SHEBOYGAN, WIS.

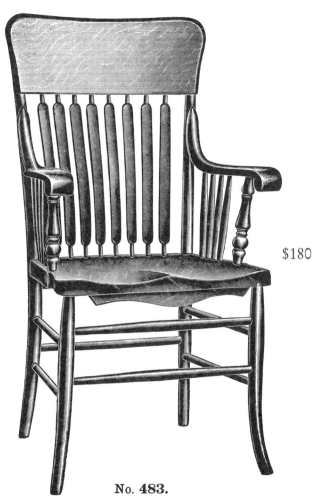

$180

No. 483.
Arm Chair.
Veneer Saddle Seat.
Golden Oak, Polished.
Weight each, 18 pounds.

$235

No. 491.
Office Chair.
Adjustable, Revolving and Tilting.
Veneer Saddle Seat.
Golden Oak, Polished.
Weight each, 40 pounds.

$275

No. 483½-B.

Settee.
43 inches long.
Veneer Seat.
Golden Oak, Polished.
Weight each, 33 pounds.

$345

No. 484-BUL.

Settee.
43 inches long.
Upholstered Dark Olive Leather Seat.
Golden Oak, Polished.
Weight each, 38 pounds.

PHOENIX CHAIR CO.
SHEBOYGAN, WIS.

$180

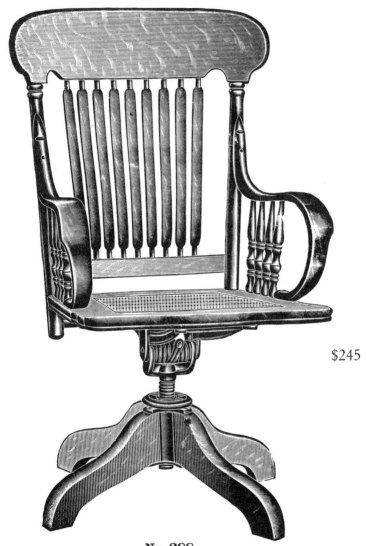

$245

No. 282.

Arm Chair.
Cane Seat.
Golden Oak, Polished.
Weight each, 18 pounds.

No. 288.

Office Chair.
Adjustable, Revolving and Tilting.
Cane Seat.
Golden Oak, Polished.
Weight each, 38 pounds.

PHOENIX CHAIR CO.
SHEBOYGAN, WIS.

$170

No. 281.

Arm Chair.
Veneer Saddle Seat.
Golden Oak, Polished.
Weight each, 19 pounds.

$235

No. 287.

Office Chair.
Adjustable, Revolving and Tilting.
Veneer Saddle Seat.
Golden Oak, Polished.
Weight each, 39 pounds.

$275

No. 281-B.

Settee.
Length, 40 inches.   Height of Back, 20 inches.
Veneer Seat.
Golden Oak, Polished.
Weight each, 42 pounds.

PHOENIX CHAIR CO.
SHEBOYGAN, WIS.

$220

No. 853½.

Arm Chair.
Quartered Oak Saddle Wood Seat.
Golden Oak, Polished.
Weight each, 15 pounds.

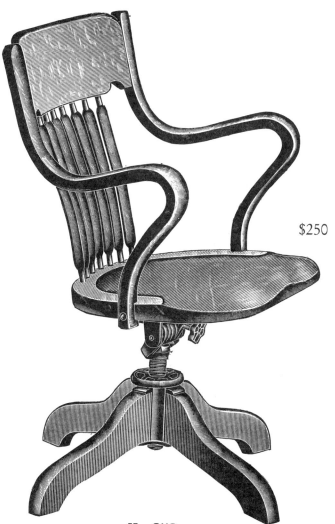

$250

No. 853.

Office Chair.
Adjustable, Revolving and Tilting.
Quartered Oak Saddle Wood Seat.
Golden Oak, Polished.
Weight each, 30 pounds.

PHOENIX CHAIR CO.
SHEBOYGAN, WIS.

$200

$240

No. 859.

Arm Chair.
Quartered Oak Saddle Wood Seat.

No. 860. Same.

Cane Seat.
Golden Oak, Polished.
Weight each, 22 pounds.

No. 861.

Office Chair.
Adjustable, Revolving and Tilting.
Quartered Oak Saddle Wood Seat.
Golden Oak, Polished.
Weight each, 41 pounds.

PHOENIX CHAIR CO.
SHEBOYGAN, WIS.

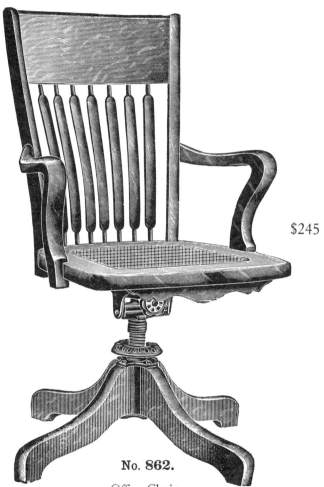

$245

No. 862.
Office Chair.
Adjustable, Revolving and Tilting.
Cane Seat.

No. 862-PL.   Same.

Dark Olive Perforated Leather Seat over Cane.
Golden Oak, Polished.
Weight each, 38 pounds.

$230

No. 862-SUL.
Office Chair.
Adjustable, Revolving and Tilting.
Upholstered Dark Olive Leather Spring Seat.
Golden Oak, Polished.
Weight each, 40 pounds.

PHOENIX CHAIR CO.
SHEBOYGAN, WIS.

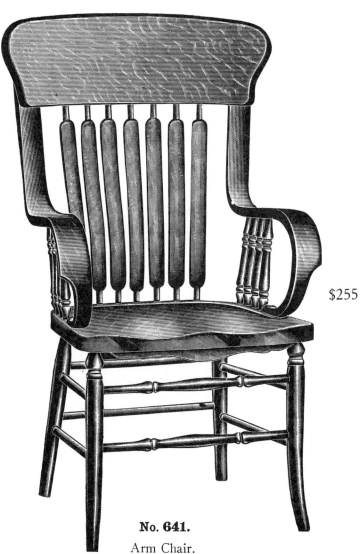

$255

No. 641.
Arm Chair.
Veneer Saddle Seat.   Rodded Arm to Seat.
Golden Oak, Polished.
Weight each, 23 pounds.

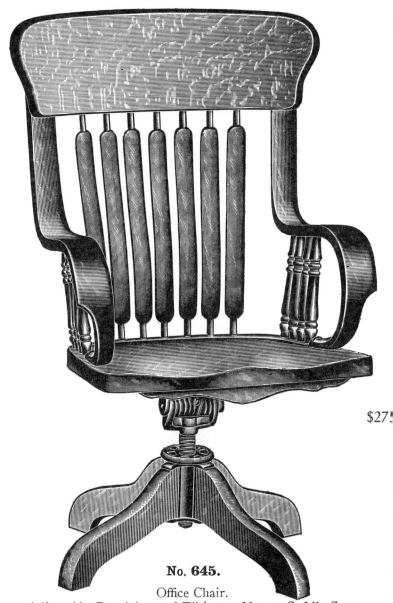

$275

No. 645.
Office Chair.
Adjustable, Revolving and Tilting.   Veneer Saddle Seat.
Rodded Arm to Seat.   Golden Oak, Polished.
Weight each, 42 pounds.

PHOENIX CHAIR CO.
SHEBOYGAN, WIS.

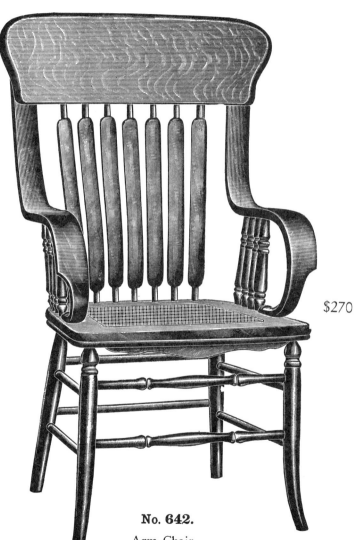

$270

No. 642.

Arm Chair.
Cane Seat.   Rodded Arm to Seat.
Golden Oak, Polished.
Weight each, 25 pounds.

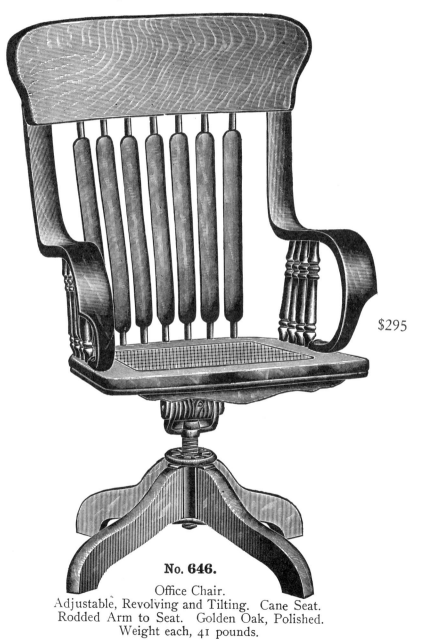

$295

No. 646.

Office Chair.
Adjustable, Revolving and Tilting.   Cane Seat.
Rodded Arm to Seat.   Golden Oak, Polished.
Weight each, 41 pounds.

PHOENIX CHAIR CO.
SHEBOYGAN, WIS.

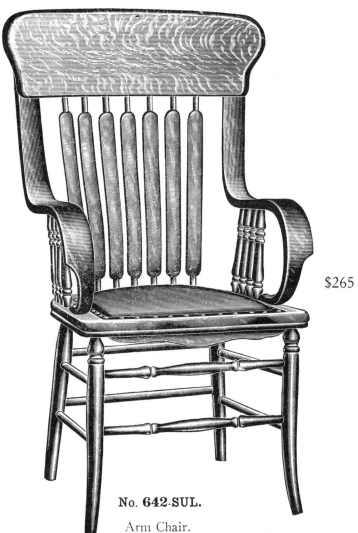

$265

No. 642-SUL.

Arm Chair.
Upholstered Dark Olive Leather Spring Seat.
Rodded Arm to Seat. Golden Oak, Polished.
Weight each, 25 pounds.

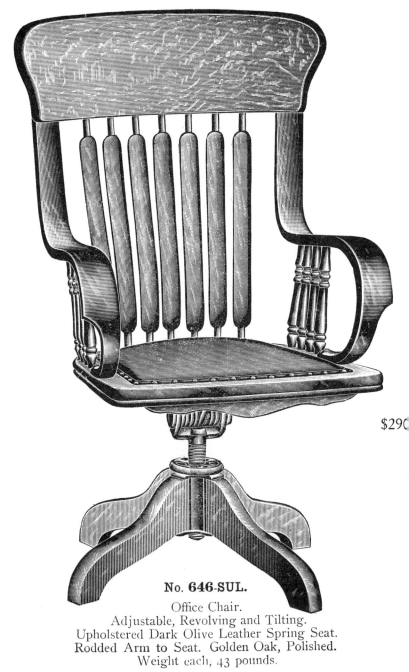

$290

No. 646-SUL.

Office Chair.
Adjustable, Revolving and Tilting.
Upholstered Dark Olive Leather Spring Seat.
Rodded Arm to Seat. Golden Oak, Polished.
Weight each, 43 pounds.

PHOENIX CHAIR CO.
SHEBOYGAN, WIS.

$200

No. 893.

Arm Chair.
Quartered Oak Saddle Wood Seat.
Golden Oak, Polished.
Weight each, 24 pounds.

$260

No. 897.

Office Chair.
Adjustable, Revolving and Tilting.
Quartered Oak Saddle Wood Seat.
Golden Oak, Polished.
Weight each, 40 pounds.

PHOENIX CHAIR CO.
SHEBOYGAN, WIS.

$220

$255

No. 871.

Arm Chair.
Quartered Oak Saddle Wood Seat.
Golden Oak, Polished.
Weight each, 22 pounds.

No. 873.

Office Chair.
Adjustable, Revolving and Tilting.
Quartered Oak Saddle Wood Seat.
Golden Oak, Polished.
Weight each, 42 pounds.

PHOENIX CHAIR CO.
SHEBOYGAN, WIS.

$245

No. 874.

Office Chair.
Adjustable, Revolving and Tilting.
Cane Seat.
Golden Oak, Polished.
Weight each, 40 pounds.

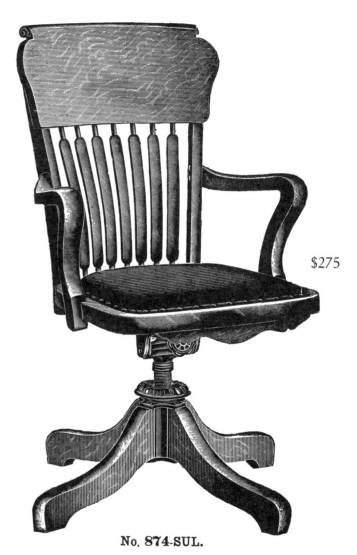

$275

No. 874-SUL.

Office Chair.
Adjustable, Revolving and Tilting.
Upholstered Dark Olive Leather Spring Seat.
Golden Oak, Polished.
Weight each, 40 pounds.

$235

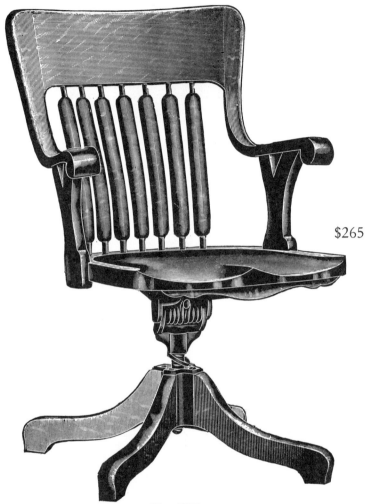

$265

No. 175.

Arm Chair.
Quartered Oak Saddle Wood Seat.

No. 175-BL. Same.

Upholstered Dark Olive Leather Back.
Golden Oak, Polished.
Weight each, 22 pounds.

No. 177.

Office Chair.
Adjustable, Revolving and Tilting.
Quartered Oak Saddle Wood Seat.

No. 177-BL. Same.

Upholstered Dark Olive Leather Back.
Golden Oak, Polished.
Weight each, 42 pounds.

PHOENIX CHAIR CO.
SHEBOYGAN, WIS.

$255

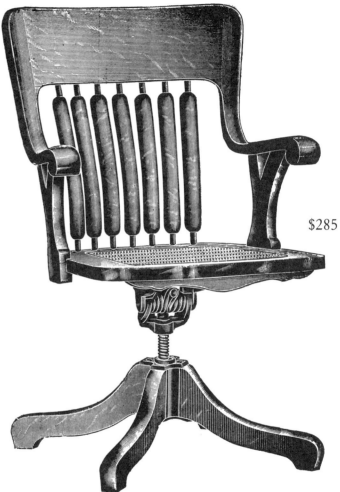

$285

No. 176.
Arm Chair.
Cane Seat.

No. 176-PL. Same.
Dark Olive Perforated Leather Seat over Cane.

No. 176-SUL. Same.
Upholstered Dark Olive Leather Spring Seat.
Golden Oak, Polished.
Weight each, 19 pounds.

No. 178.
Office Chair.
Adjustable, Revolving and Tilting.
Cane Seat.

No. 178-PL. Same.
Dark Olive Perforated Leather Seat over Cane.
Golden Oak, Polished.
Weight each, 39 pounds.

PHOENIX CHAIR CO.
SHEBOYGAN, WIS.

$250

$275

No. 176-PBL.
Arm Chair.

Upholstered Dark Olive Leather Back and Perforated Leather
Seat over Cane.

No. 176-SUBL.   Same.

Upholstered Dark Olive Leather Back and Spring Seat.
Golden Oak, Polished.
Weight each, 19 pounds.

No. 178-PBL.

Office Chair.
Adjustable, Revolving and Tilting.
Upholstered Dark Olive Leather Back and Perforated Leather
Seat over Cane.
Golden Oak, Polished.
Weight each, 42 pounds.

PHOENIX CHAIR CO.
SHEBOYGAN, WIS.

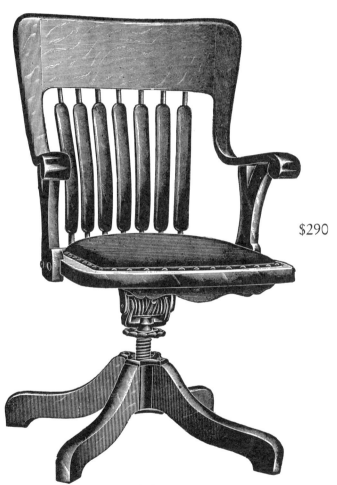

$290

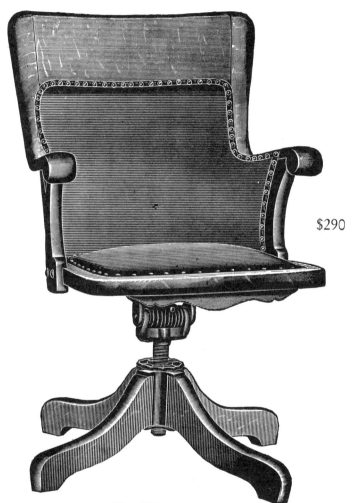

$290

No. 178-SUL.

Office Chair.
Adjustable, Revolving and Tilting.
Upholstered Dark Olive Leather Spring Seat.
Golden Oak, Polished.
Weight each, 40 pounds.

No. 178-SUBL.

Office Chair.
Adjustable, Revolving and Tilting.
Upholstered Dark Olive Leather Back and Spring Seat.
Golden Oak, Polished.
Weight each, 42 pounds.

PHOENIX CHAIR CO.
SHEBOYGAN, WIS.

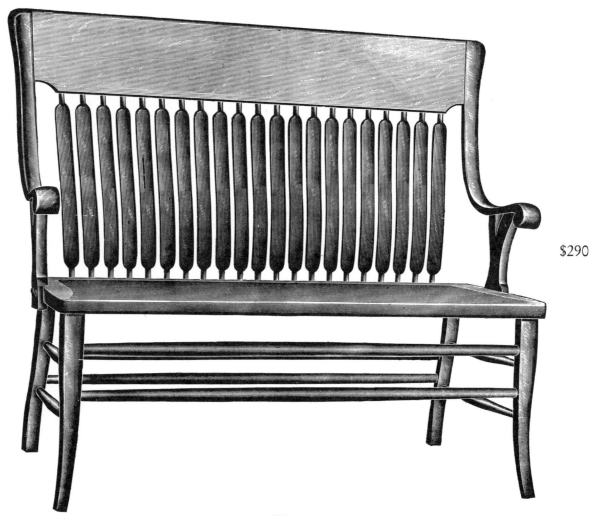

$290

No. 175-B.

Settee.
43 inches long.
Quartered Oak Wood Seat.
Golden Oak, Polished.
Weight each, 48 pounds.

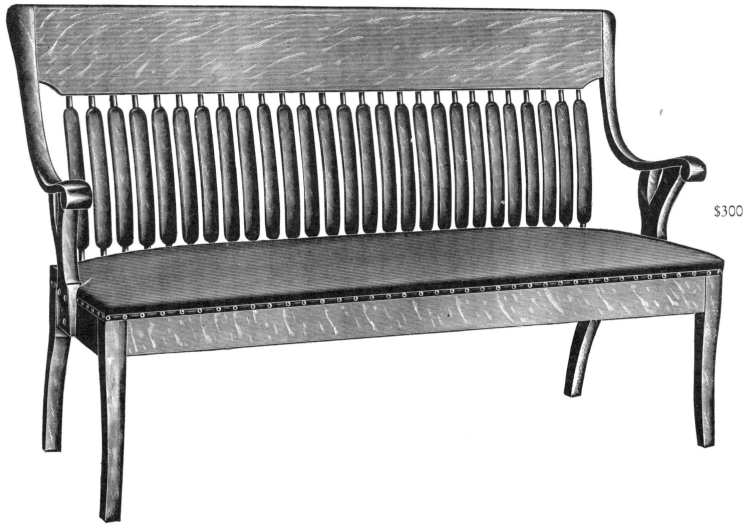

$300

No. 176½-BSUL.

Settee.
5 feet long.
Upholstered Dark Olive Leather Spring Seat,
Golden Oak, Polished.
Weight each, 62 pounds.

$245

No. 831.

Arm Chair.
Quartered Oak Saddle Wood Seat.
Golden Oak, Polished.
Weight each, 25 pounds.

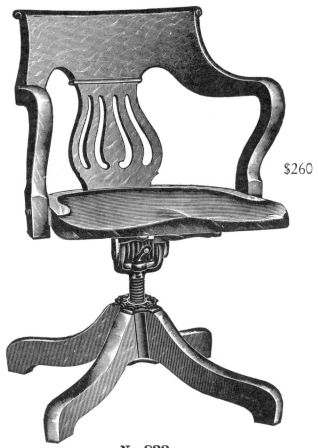

$260

No. 833.

Office Chair.
Adjustable, Revolving and Tilting.
Quartered Oak Saddle Wood Seat.
Golden Oak, Polished.
Weight each, 42 pounds.

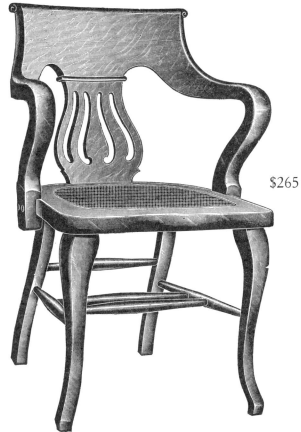

$265

No. 832.

Arm Chair.
Cane Seat.

No. 832-PL. Same.

Dark Olive Perforated Leather Seat over Cane
Golden Oak, Polished.
Weight each, 20 pounds.

$280

No. 834.

Office Chair.
Adjustable, Revolving and Tilting.
Cane Seat.

No. 834-PL. Same.

With Dark Olive Perforated Leather Seat over Cane.
Golden Oak, Polished.
Weight each, 38 pounds.

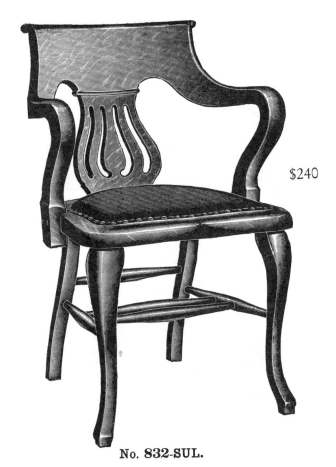

$240

No. 832-SUL.

Arm Chair.
Upholstered Dark Olive Leather Spring Seat.
Golden Oak, Polished.
Weight each, 21 pounds.

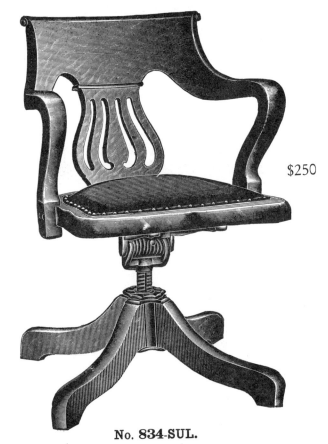

$250

No. 834-SUL.

Office Chair.
Adjustable, Revolving and Tilting.
Upholstered Dark Olive Leather Spring Seat.
Golden Oak, Polished.
Weight each, 40 pounds.

$250

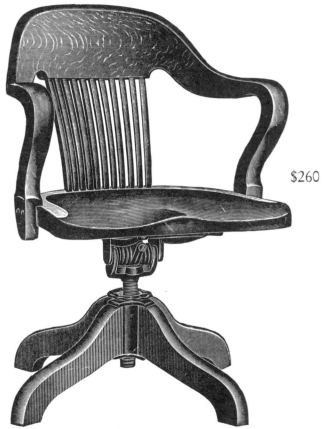

$260

No. 867.

Arm Chair.
Quartered Oak Saddle Wood Seat.

No. 868. Same.
Cane Seat.
Golden Oak, Polished.
Weight each, 22 pounds.

No. 869.

Office Chair.
Adjustable, Revolving and Tilting.
Quartered Oak Saddle Wood Seat.

No. 870. Same.
Cane Seat. Golden Oak, Polished.
Weight each, 39 pounds.

$255

No. 868-PL.

Arm Chair.
Dark Olive Perforated Leather Seat over Cane.
Golden Oak, Polished.
Weight each, 21 pounds.

$265

No. 870-PL.

Office Chair.
Adjustable, Revolving and Tilting.
Dark Olive Perforated Leather Seat over Cane.
Golden Oak, Polished.
Weight each, 39 pounds.

PHOENIX CHAIR CO.
SHEBOYGAN, WIS.

$240

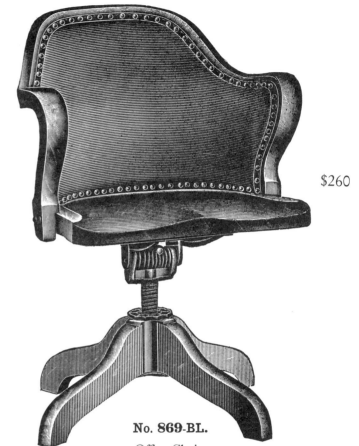

$260

No. 867-BL.

Arm Chair.
Quartered Oak Saddle Wood Seat.
Upholstered Dark Olive Leather Back.

No. 868-BL. Same.

Cane Seat.
With Upholstered Dark Olive Leather Back.

No. 868-PBL. Same.

Upholstered Dark Olive Leather Back and Perforated Leather
Seat over Cane.
Golden Oak, Polished.
Weight each, 23 pounds.

No. 869-BL.

Office Chair.
Adjustable, Revolving and Tilting.
Quartered Oak Saddle Wood Seat.
Upholstered Dark Olive Leather Back.

No. 870-BL. Same.

Cane Seat.
Upholstered Dark Olive Leather Back.

No. 870-PBL. Same.

Upholstered Dark Olive Leather Back and Perforated Leather
Seat over Cane.
Golden Oak, Polished.
Weight each, 39 pounds.

PHOENIX CHAIR CO.
SHEBOYGAN, WIS.

$220

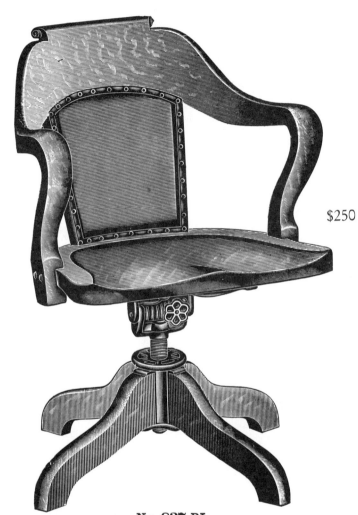

$250

No. 835-BL.

Arm Chair.
Quartered Oak Saddle Wood Seat.
Upholstered Dark Olive Leather Back.
Golden Oak, Polished.
Weight each, 24 pounds.

No. 837-BL.

Office Chair.
Adjustable, Revolving and Tilting.
Quartered Oak Saddle Wood Seat.
Upholstered Dark Olive Leather Back.
Golden Oak, Polished.
Weight each, 42 pounds.

PHOENIX CHAIR CO.
SHEBOYGAN, WIS.

$235

$265

No. 836-SUBL.

Arm Chair.
Upholstered Dark Olive Leather Back and Spring Seat.
Golden Oak, Polished.
Weight each, 22 pounds.

No. 838-SUBL.

Office Chair.
Adjustable, Revolving and Tilting.
Upholstered Dark Olive Leather Back and Spring Seat.
Golden Oak, Polished.
Weight each, 42 pounds.

$240

No. 1131-HBL.

Arm Chair.
Upholstered Dark Olive Leather Back and Spring Seat.
Golden Oak, Polished.
Weight each, 23 pounds.

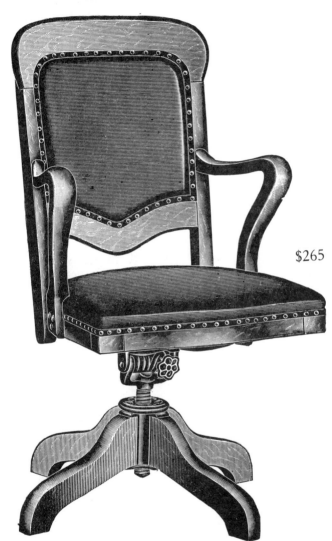

$265

No. 1133-HBL.

Office Chair.
Adjustable, Revolving and Tilting.
Upholstered Dark Olive Leather Back and Spring Seat.
Golden Oak, Polished.
Weight each, 37 pounds.

$320

No. 1134-HBL.

Settee.
Length, 40 inches.
Upholstered Dark Olive Leather Back and Spring Seat.
Mahogany Finish, Polished.
Golden Oak, Polished.
Weight each, 40 pounds.

PHOENIX CHAIR CO.
SHEBOYGAN, WIS.

$160

No. 675.
Desk Chair.
Adjustable, Revolving and Tilting.
Wood Seat.
Golden Elm, Gloss.
Weight each, 30 pounds.

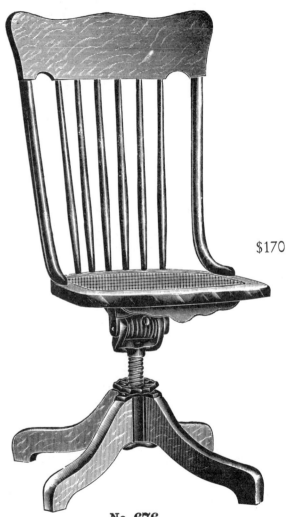

$170

No. 676.
Desk Chair.
Adjustable, Revolving and Tilting.
Cane Seat.
Golden Elm, Gloss.
Weight each, 28 pounds.

PHOENIX CHAIR CO.
SHEBOYGAN, WIS.

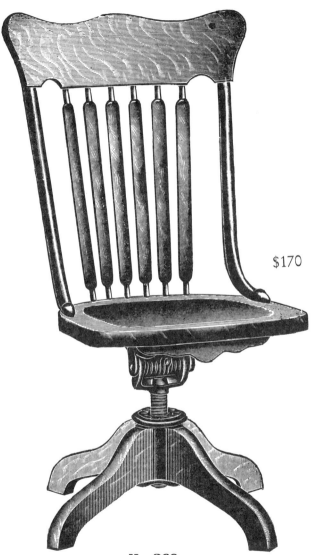

$170

No. 369.
Desk Chair.
Adjustable, Revolving and Tilting.
Wood Seat. Golden Elm, Gloss.
Weight each, 30 pounds.

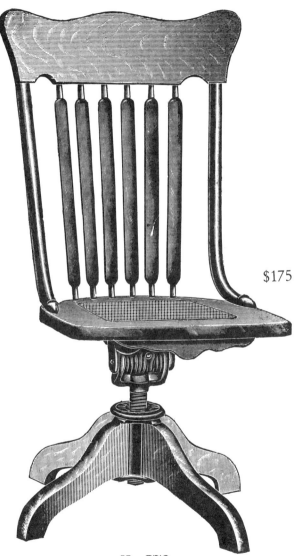

$175

No. 370.
Desk Chair.
Adjustable, Revolving and Tilting.
Cane Seat. Golden Elm, Gloss.
Weight each, 28 pounds.

PHOENIX CHAIR CO.
SHEBOYGAN, WIS,

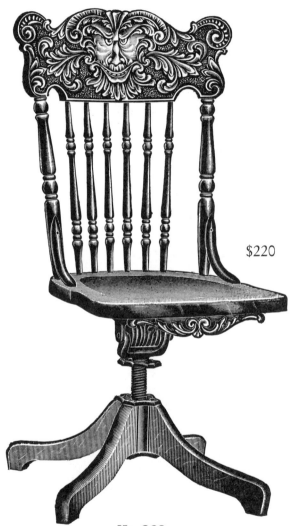

$220

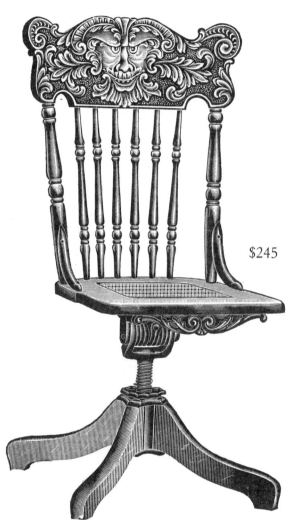

$245

No. 269.

Desk Chair.
Adjustable, Revolving and Tilting.
Wood Seat.
Golden Elm, Gloss.
Weight each, 29 pounds.

No. 270.

Desk Chair.
Adjustable, Revolving and Tilting.
Cane Seat.
Golden Elm, Gloss.
Weight each, 27 pounds.

PHOENIX CHAIR CO.
SHEBOYGAN, WIS.

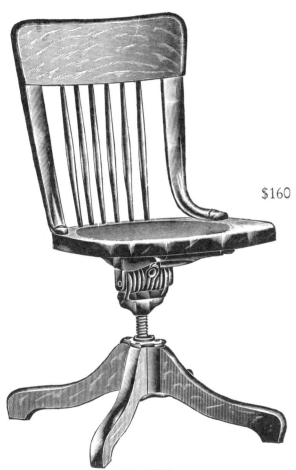

$160

No. 135.

Desk Chair.
Adjustable, Revolving and Tilting.
Wood Seat.
Golden Elm, Gloss.
Weight each, 30 pounds.

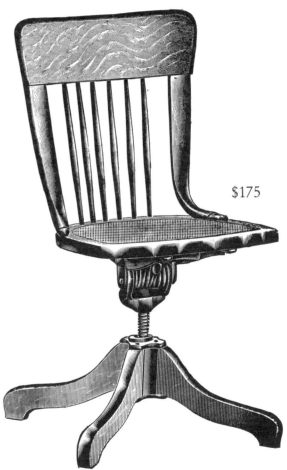

$175

No. 136.

Desk Chair.
Adjustable, Revolving and Tilting.
Cane Seat.
Golden Elm, Gloss.
Weight each, 27 pounds.

PHOENIX CHAIR CO.
SHEBOYGAN, WIS.

$160

No. 65.

Desk Chair.
Adjustable, Revolving and Tilting.
Veneer Seat.
Golden Oak, Polished.
Weight each, 29 pounds.

$175

No. 66.

Desk Chair.
Cane Seat.

No. 66-UL. Same.

Upholstered Dark Olive Leather Seat.
Golden Oak, Polished.
Weight each, 28 pounds.

PHOENIX CHAIR CO.
SHEBOYGAN, WIS.

$160

$175

No. 285.

Desk Chair.
Adjustable, Revolving and Tilting.
Veneer Saddle Seat.
Golden Oak, Polished.
Weight each, 30 pounds.

No. 286.

Desk Chair.
Adjustable, Revolving and Tilting.
Cane Seat.
Golden Oak, Polished.
Weight each, 29 pounds.

PHOENIX CHAIR CO.
SHEBOYGAN, WIS.

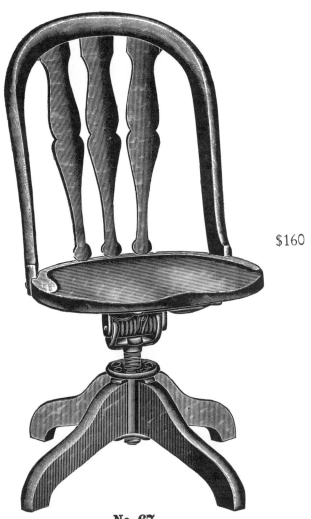

$160

No. 67.
Desk Chair.
Adjustable, Revolving and Tilting.
Veneer Saddle Seat.
Golden Oak, Polished.
Weight each, 29 pounds.

$165

No. 57.
Desk Chair.
Veneer Saddle Seat.
Golden Oak, Polished.
Weight each, 29 pounds.

$170

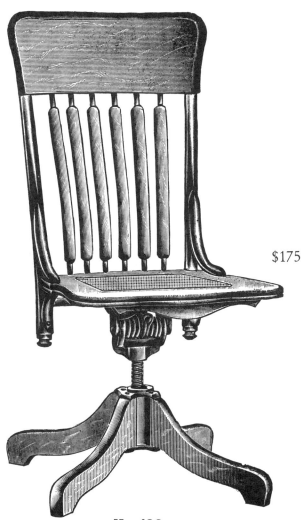

$175

No. 489.

Desk Chair.
Adjustable, Revolving and Tilting.
Veneer Saddle Seat.
Golden Oak, Polished.
Weight each 32 pounds.

No. 490.

Desk Chair.
Adjustable, Revolving and Tilting.
Cane Seat.
Golden Oak, Polished.
Weight each, 30 pounds.

PHOENIX CHAIR CO.
SHEBOYGAN, WIS.

$175

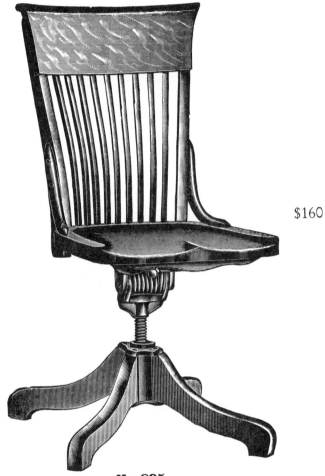

$160

No. 896.

Desk Chair.
Adjustable, Revolving and Tilting.

No. 896-PL. Same.

Dark Olive Perforated Leather Seat over Cane.
Golden Oak, Polished.
Weight each, 30 pounds.

No. 895.

Desk Chair.
Adjustable, Revolving and Tilting.
Quartered Oak Saddle Wood Seat.
Golden Oak, Polished.
Weight each, 32 pounds.

PHOENIX CHAIR CO.
SHEBOYGAN, WIS.

$165

No. 896-UL.

Desk Chair.
Adjustable, Revolving and Tilting.
Upholstered Dark Olive Leather Seat.
Golden Oak, Polished.
Weight each, 31 pounds.

$165

No. 490-UL.

Desk Chair.
Adjustable, Revolving and Tilting.
Upholstered Dark Olive Leather Seat.
Golden Oak, Polished.
Weight each, 32 pounds.

$160

No. 139.
Desk Chair.
Adjustable, Revolving and Tilting.
Quartered Oak Saddle Wood Seat.
Golden Oak, Polished.
Weight each, 30 pounds.

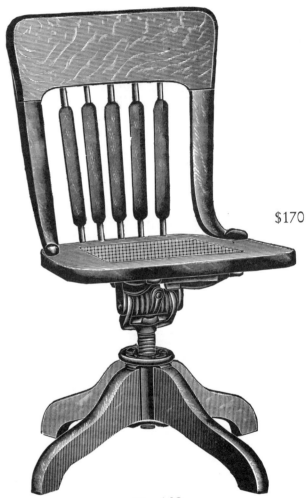

$170

No. 140.
Desk Chair.
Adjustable, Revolving and Tilting.
Cane Seat.
Golden Oak, Polished.
Weight each, 29 pounds.

PHOENIX CHAIR CO.
SHEBOYGAN, WIS.

$170

No. 141.

Desk Chair.
-Adjustable, Revolving and Tilting.
Veneer Saddle Seat.
Golden Oak, Polished.
Weight each, 30 pounds.

$170

No. 142.

Desk Chair.
Adjustable, Revolving and Tilting.
Cane Seat.

No. 142-PL.   Same.

Dark Olive Perforated Leather Seat over Cane.
Golden Oak, Polished.
Weight each, 29 pounds.

PHOENIX CHAIR CO.
SHEBOYGAN, WIS.

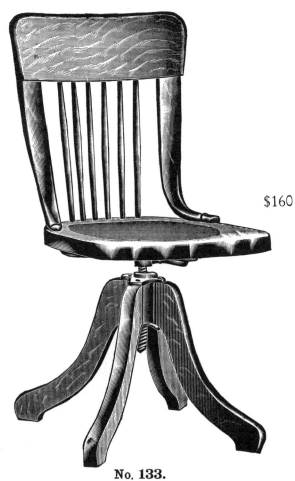

$160

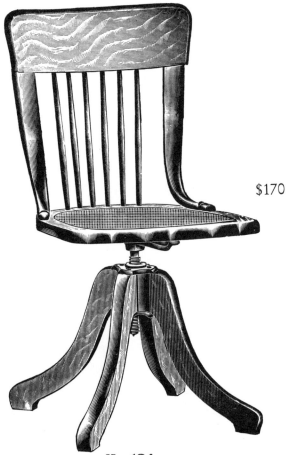

$170

No. 133.

Typewriter Chair.
Adjustable and Revolving.
Wood Seat.
Golden Elm, Gloss.
Weight each, 22 pounds.

No. 134.

Typewriter Chair.
Adjustable and Revolving.
Cane Seat.
Golden Elm, Gloss.
Weight each, 20 pounds.

PHOENIX CHAIR CO.
SHEBOYGAN, WIS.

$125

No. 59.

Typewriter Chair.
Adjustable and Revolving.
Veneer Seat.
Golden Oak, Polished.
Weight each, 19 pounds.

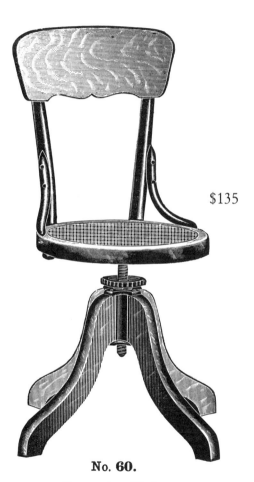

$135

No. 60.

Typewriter Chair.
Adjustable and Revolving.
Cane Seat.
Golden Oak, Polished.
Weight each, 19 pounds.

PHOENIX CHAIR CO.
SHEBOYGAN, WIS.

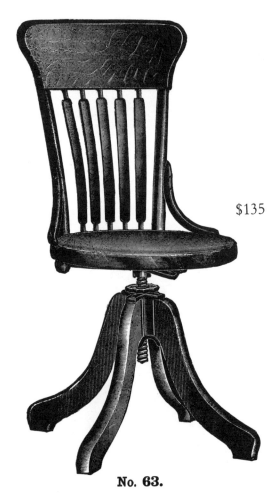

$135

No. 63.

Typewriter Chair.
Adjustable and Revolving.
Veneer Seat.
Golden Oak, Polished.
Weight each, 22 pounds.

$145

No. 64.

Typewriter Chair.
Adjustable and Revolving.
Cane Seat.

No. 64-UL. Same.

Upholstered Dark Olive Leather Seat.
Golden Oak, Polished.
Weight each, 21 pounds.

PHOENIX CHAIR CO.
SHEBOYGAN, WIS.

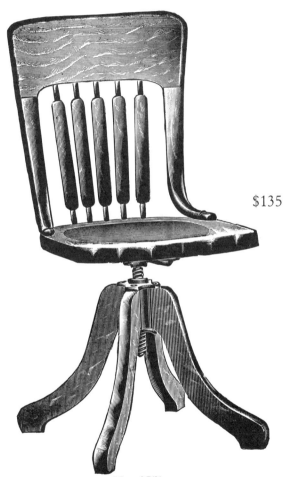

$135

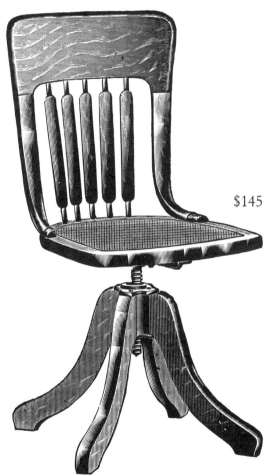

$145

No. 137.

Typewriter Chair.
Adjustable and Revolving.
Quartered Oak Saddle Wood Seat.
Golden Oak, Polished.
Weight each, 25 pounds.

No. 138.

Typewriter Chair.
Adjustable and Revolving.
Cane Seat.
Golden Oak, Polished.
Weight each, 21 pounds.

PHOENIX CHAIR CO.
SHEBOYGAN, WIS.

$110

No 85.
Typewriter Chair.
Adjustable and Revolving, with Adjustable Spring Back.
Veneer Seat.
Golden Elm, Gloss.
Golden Oak, Polished.
Weight each, 22 pounds.

$110

No. 85-BL.
Typewriter Chair.
Adjustable and Revolving, with Adjustable Spring Back.
Veneer Seat.
Upholstered Dark Olive Leather Back.
Golden Elm, Gloss.
Golden Oak, Polished.
Weight each, 22 pounds.

PHOENIX CHAIR CO.
SHEBOYGAN, WIS.

$120

No. 86-PL.

Typewriter Chair.
Adjustable and Revolving, with Adjustable Spring Back.
Dark Olive Perforated Leather Seat over Cane.

No. 86. Same.

Cane Seat.
Golden Elm, Gloss.
Golden Oak, Polished.
Weight each, 22 pounds.

$120

No. 86-UBL.

Typewriter Chair.
Adjustable and Revolving, with Adjustable Spring Back.
Upholstered Dark Olive Leather Back and Seat.
Golden Elm, Gloss.
Golden Oak, Polished.
Weight each, 24 pounds.

PHOENIX CHAIR CO.
SHEBOYGAN, WIS.

$150

No. 331.

Revolving Desk Stool.
31 inches High.
Wood Seat.
Golden Elm, Gloss.
Weight each, 14 pounds.

$150

No. 331-R.

Revolving Desk Stool.
Circular Foot Rest.
31 inches High.
Wood Seat.
Golden Elm, Gloss.
Weight each, 15 pounds.

PHOENIX CHAIR CO.
SHEBOYGAN, WIS.

$170

$170

No. 332.

Revolving Desk Stool.
31 inches High.
Cane Seat.
Golden Elm, Gloss.
Weight each, 15 pounds.

No. 332-R.

Revolving Desk Stool.
Circular Foot Rest.
31 inches High.
Cane Seat.
Golden Elm, Gloss.
Weight each, 16 pounds.

$160

No. 333.

Desk Stool.
Adjustable and Revolving.
30 to 34 inches High.
Wood Seat.
Golden Elm, Gloss.
Weight each, 16 pounds.

$160

No. 333-R.

Desk Stool.
Adjustable and Revolving.
Circular Foot Rest.
30 to 34 inches High.
Wood Seat.
Golden Elm, Gloss.
Weight each, 17 pounds.

PHOENIX CHAIR CO.
SHEBOYGAN, WIS.

$170

No. 334.

Desk Stool.
Adjustable and Revolving.
30 to 34 inches High.
Cane Seat.
Golden Elm, Gloss.
Weight each, 15 pounds.

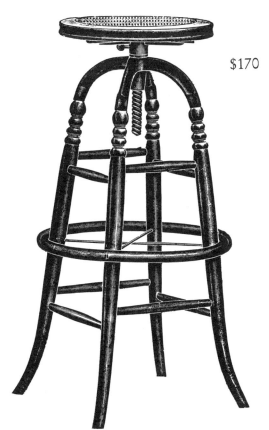

$170

No. 334-R.

Desk Stool.
Adjustable and Revolving.
Circular Foot Rest.
30 to 34 inches High.
Cane Seat.
Golden Elm, Gloss.
Weight each, 16 pounds.

PHOENIX CHAIR CO.
SHEBOYGAN, WIS.

$150

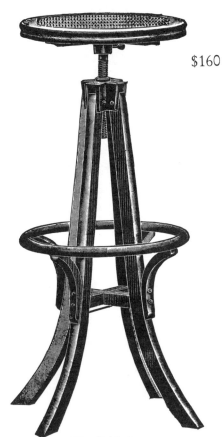

$160

No. 341-R.

Desk Stool.
Adjustable and Revolving.
31 to 36 inches High.
Quartered Oak Wood Seat.
Golden Oak, Polished.
Weight each, 17 pounds.

No. 342-R.

Desk Stool.
Adjustable and Revolving.
31 to 36 inches High.
Cane Seat.
Golden Oak, Polished.
Weight each, 16 pounds.

PHOENIX CHAIR CO.
SHEBOYGAN, WIS.

$170

No. 546.

Vienna Desk Stool.
Adjustable and Revolving.
Cane Seat.
Golden Oak, Polished.
Weight each, 17 pounds.

$170

No. 547.

Vienna Desk Stool.
Adjustable and Revolving.
Cane Seat.
Golden Oak, Polished.
Weight each, 18 pounds.

$180

$180

No. 335.

Desk Stool.

Adjustable and Revolving.
30 to 34 inches High.
Wood Seat.
Golden Elm, Gloss.
Weight each, 22 pounds.

No. 335-R.

Desk Stool.
Adjustable and Revolving.
30 to 34 inches High.
Circular Foot Rest.
Golden Elm, Gloss.
Weight each, 23 pounds.

$210

No. 9¼.

Desk Stool.
Adjustable and Revolving.
30 to 34 inches High.
Veneer Seat.
Golden Oak, Polished.
Weight each, 20 pounds.

$225

No. 9½.

Desk Stool.
Adjustable and Revolving.
30 to 34 inches High.
Cane Seat.
Golden Oak, Polished.
Weight each, 20 pounds.

$175

No. 337-R.

Desk Stool.
Adjustable and Revolving.
30 to 34 inches High.
Quartered Oak Saddle Wood Seat.
Golden Oak, Polished.
Weight each, 25 pounds.

$195

No. 338-R.

Desk Stool.
Adjustable and Revolving.
30 to 34 inches High.
Cane Seat.
Golden Oak, Polished.
Weight each, 23 pounds.

$215

No. 548½.

Vienna Desk Stool.
Adjustable and Revolving.
32 to 35 inches High.
Veneer Seat.
Golden Oak, Polished.
Weight each, 20 pounds.

$225

No. 548.

Vienna Desk Stool.
Adjustable and Revolving.
32 to 35 inches High.
Cane Seat.
Golden Oak, Polished.
Weight each, 20 pounds.

$215

No. 549½.

Vienna Desk Stool.
Adjustable and Revolving.
32 to 35 inches High.
Veneer Seat and Cane Back.
Golden Oak, Polished.
Weight each, 22 pounds.

$225

No. 549.

Vienna Desk Stool.
Adjustable and Revolving.
32 to 35 inches High.
Cane Seat and Back.
Golden Oak, Polished.
Weight each, 22 pounds.

$110

$125

No. 321.

Stool.
18 inches High.
Wood Seat.
Golden Elm, Gloss.
Weight each, 6 pounds.

No. 322.

Stool.
18 inches High.
Cane Seat.
Golden Elm, Gloss.
Weight each, 5 pounds.

PHOENIX CHAIR CO.
SHEBOYGAN, WIS.

$120

No. 323.
Stool.
24 inches High.
Wood Seat.
Golden Elm, Gloss.
Weight each, 7 pounds.

$135

No. 324.
Stool.
24 inches High.
Cane Seat.
Golden Elm, Gloss.
Weight each, 6 pounds.

PHOENIX CHAIR CO.
SHEBOYGAN, WIS.

$150

$150

No. 325.

Desk Stool.
33 inches High.
Wood Seat.
Golden Elm, Gloss.
Weight each, 8 pounds.

No. 325-R.

Desk Stool.
33 inches High.
Wood Seat.
Golden Elm, Gloss.
Weight each, 9 pounds.

PHOENIX CHAIR CO.
SHEBOYGAN, WIS.

$155

No. 326.

Desk Stool.
33 inches High.
Cane Seat.
Golden Elm, Gloss.
Weight each, 8 pounds.

$155

No. 326-R.

Desk Stool.
33 inches High.
Cane Seat.
Golden Elm, Gloss.
Weight each, 9 pounds.

PHOENIX CHAIR CO.
SHEBOYGAN, WIS.

$100

No. 541½.

Vienna Store Stool.
Veneer Seat.
18 inches High.
Golden Oak, Polished.
Weight each, 7 pounds.

$110

No. 541.

Vienna Store Stool.
Cane Seat.
18 inches High.
Golden Oak, Polished.
Weight each, 6 pounds.

$110

$125

No. 542½.

Vienna Store Stool.
Veneer Seat.
24 inches High.
Golden Oak, Polished.
Weight each, 8 pounds.

No. 542.

Vienna Store Stool.
Cane Seat.
24 inches High.
Golden Oak, Polished.
Weight each, 7 pounds.

PHOENIX CHAIR CO.
SHEBOYGAN, WIS.

$110

No. 543½.

Vienna Desk Stool.
30 inches High.
Veneer Seat.
Golden Oak, Polished.
Weight each, 9 pounds.

$120

No. 543.

Vienna Desk Stool.
30 inches High.
Cane Seat.
Golden Oak, Polished.
Weight each, 8 pounds.

PHOENIX CHAIR CO.
SHEBOYGAN, WIS.

$110

No. 544½.

Vienna Desk Stool.
Veneer Seat.
33 inches High.
Golden Oak, Polished.
Weight each, 11 pounds.

$120

No. 544.

Vienna Desk Stool.
Cane Seat.
33 inches High.
Golden Oak, Polished.
Weight each, 10 pounds.

PHOENIX CHAIR CO.
SHEBOYGAN, WIS.

$110

No. 318.

Counter Stool.
12 inches diameter.
Quartered Oak Wood Seat.
Japanned Iron Pedestal.
21 inches High.   Weight each, 10 pounds.
25 inches High.   Weight each, 11 pounds.
30 inches High.   Weight each, 12 pounds.
Golden Oak, Polished.

$120

No. 318-R.

Counter Stool.
12 inches diameter.
Quartered Oak Wood Seat, with Nickeled Rim.
Japanned Iron Pedestal.
21 inches High.   Weight each, 12 pounds.
25 inches High.   Weight each, 13 pounds.
30 inches High.   Weight each, 14 pounds.
Golden Oak, Polished.

PHOENIX CHAIR CO.
SHEBOYGAN, WIS.

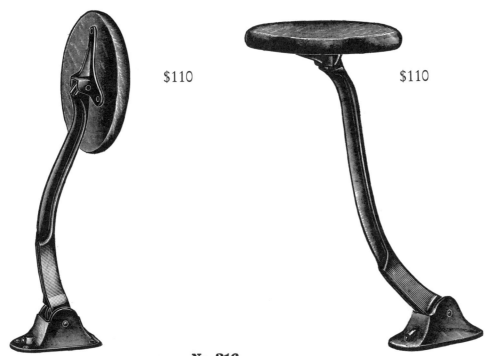

$110 $110

$110

No. 316.

Automatic Folding Counter Stool.
21 inches High, for Counter 30 to 33 inches High.

No. 317. Same.

For Counter 36 to 38 inches High.
Quartered Golden Oak Top, 12 inches Diameter.
Golden Oak, Polished.
Japanned Iron Pedestal.
Weight each, 15 pounds.

No. 318½.

Counter Stool.
Quartered Oak Wood Seat.
12 inches Diameter.
Japanned Iron Pedestal.
21 inches High.
25 inches High.
30 inches High.
Golden Oak, Polished.
Weight each, 16 pounds.

PHOENIX CHAIR CO.
SHEBOYGAN, WIS.

$140

No. 319.

Counter Stool.
Quartered Oak Wood Seat.
12 inches Diameter.
Japanned Iron Pedestal.
Golden Oak, Polished.
21 inches High.
25 inches High.
30 inches High.
Weight each, 18 pounds.

$140

No. 319-R.

Counter Stool.
Quartered Oak Wood Seat.
12 inches Diameter.
Japanned Iron Pedestal.
Golden Oak, Polished.
21 inches High.
25 inches High.
30 inches High.
Weight each, 18 pounds.

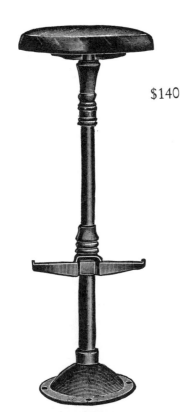

$140

No. 318-L.

Lunch Counter Stool with Foot Rest.
Quartered Oak Wood Seat.
12 inches Diameter.
Japanned Iron Pedestal.
26 inches High, or over.
Golden Oak, Polished.
Weight each, 13 pounds.

$135

No. 319½-L.

Lunch Counter Stool with Foot Rest.
Quartered Oak Wood Seat.
12 inches Diameter.
Japanned Iron Pedestal.
33 inches High, only.
Golden Oak, Polished.
Weight each, 19 pounds.

$150

No. 335-L.

Lunch Counter Stool, with Foot Rest.
Golden Elm, Gloss.
Japanned Iron Pedestal.
26 inches High, or over.
Weight each, 24 pounds.

$150

No. 597-L.

Lunch Counter Stool, with Foot Rest
Japanned Iron Pedestal.
Veneer Seat.
Golden Oak, Gloss.
33 inches High, only.
Weight each, 34 pounds.

$145

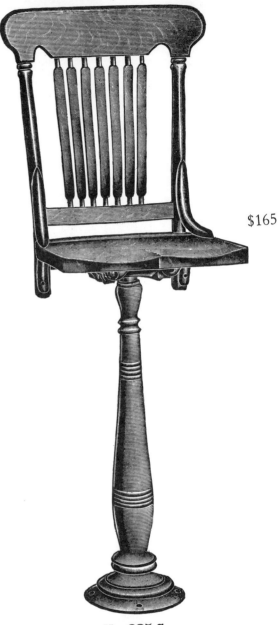

$165

No. 361-S.

Lunch Counter Stool.
Wood Seat.
Golden Elm, Gloss.
Japanned Iron Pedestal.
17 inches High.
25 inches High.
30 inches High.
Weight each, 27 pounds.

No. 285-S.

Lunch Counter Stool.
Veneer Saddle Seat.
Golden Oak, Polished.
Japanned Iron Pedestal.
17 inches High.
25 inches High.
30 inches High.
Weight each, 26 pounds.

PHOENIX CHAIR CO.
SHEBOYGAN, WIS.

$145

$175

No. 335-S.

Shoe Store Stool.
Golden Elm, Gloss.
Japanned Iron Pedestal.
17 inches High.
Weight each, 21 pounds.

No. 179-JPL.

Jury Chair, Revolving and Tilting, or Tilting only.
Japanned Iron Pedestal.
Dark Olive Perforated Leather, over Cane.
Golden Oak, Polished:
Weight each, 42 pounds.
This Jury Base can be furnished under any Office Chair Top without
extra charge.
If wanted without tilting device, deduct $6.00 per dozen.

PHOENIX CHAIR CO.
SHEBOYGAN, WIS.

$200

No. 246.

Lawn Chair.
Red, Green or Golden Elm, Gloss.
Weight each, 18 pounds.

$200

No. 247.

Lawn Rocker.
Red, Green or Golden Elm, Gloss.
Weight each, 20 pounds.

PHOENIX CHAIR CO.
SHEBOYGAN, WIS.

$225

No. 188.

Lawn Chair.
Red, Green or Golden Elm, Gloss.
Weight each, 18 pounds.

$245

No. 189.

Lawn Rocker.
Red, Green or Golden Elm, Gloss.
Weight each, 21 pounds.

PHOENIX CHAIR CO.
SHEBOYGAN, WIS.

$210

$295

No. 1011.

Veranda Chair, Slat Seat.
Red, Green or Golden Elm, Gloss.
Rodded Arm to Rack.
Weight each, 20 pounds.

No. 1011½.

Veranda Rocker, Slat Seat.
Red, Green or Golden Elm, Gloss.
Rodded Arm to Rack.
Weight each, 22 pounds.

$255

No. 1010.

Veranda Settee, Slat Seat.
43 inches Long.
Red, Green or Golden Elm, Gloss.
Rodded Arm to Rack.
Weight each, 30 pounds.

$310

No. 1010½.

Veranda Rocker, Slat Seat.
43 inches Long.
Red, Green or Golden Elm, Gloss.
Rodded Arm to Rack.
Weight each, 31 pounds.

PHOENIX CHAIR CO.
SHEBOYGAN, WIS.

$150

No. 53.

Veranda Chair.
Double Cane Seat.
Green, Red or Golden Elm, Gloss.
Rodded Arm to Rack.
Weight each, 20 pounds.

$185

No. 54.

Veranda Rocker.
Double Cane Seat.
Green, Red or Golden Elm, Gloss.
Rodded Arm to Rack.
Weight each, 25 pounds.

PHOENIX CHAIR CO.
SHEBOYGAN, WIS.

$290

No. 160.

Lawn Settee.

No. 160.	4 feet Long.	Weight 28 pounds.
No. 160.	5 feet Long.	Weight 34 pounds.
No. 160.	6 feet Long.	Weight 39 pounds.
No. 160.	8 feet Long.	Weight 50 pounds.
No. 160.	10 feet Long.	Weight 60 pounds.

Red, Green or Golden Elm, Gloss.

PHOENIX CHAIR CO.
SHEBOYGAN, WIS.

$235

No. 363-B.

Settee.
40 inches Long.
Height of Back, 23 inches.
Veneer Seat.
Golden Elm, Gloss.
Weight each, 25 pounds.

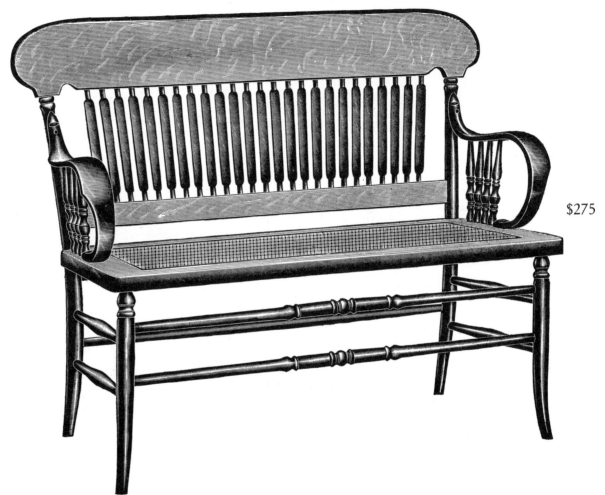

$275

No. 282-B.

Settée.
43 inches Long.
Height of Back, 20 inches.
Golden Oak, Polished.
Weight each, 40 pounds.

$235

No. 281-B.

Settee.
43 inches Long.
Veneer Seat.
Golden Oak, Polished.
Weight each, 42 pounds.

$210

No. 484-B.

Settee.
43 inches Long.
Cane Seat.
Golden Oak, Polished.
Weight each, 33 pounds.

$210

No. 483½-B.

Settee.
43 inches Long.
Veneer Seat.
Golden Oak, Polished.
Weight each, 33 pounds.

PHOENIX CHAIR CO.
SHEBOYGAN, WIS.

$210

No. 484-BUL.

Settee.
43 inches Long.
Upholstered Dark Olive Leather Seat.
Golden Oak, Polished.
Weight each, 38 pounds.

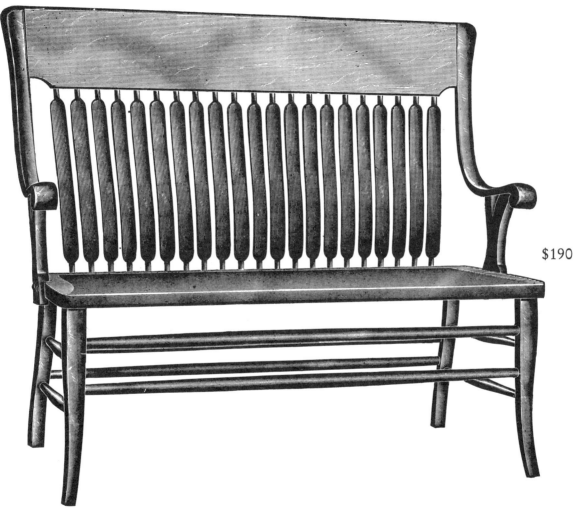

$190

No. 175-B.

Settee.
43 inches Long.
Quartered Oak Wood Seat.
Golden Oak, Polished.
Weight each, 48 pounds.

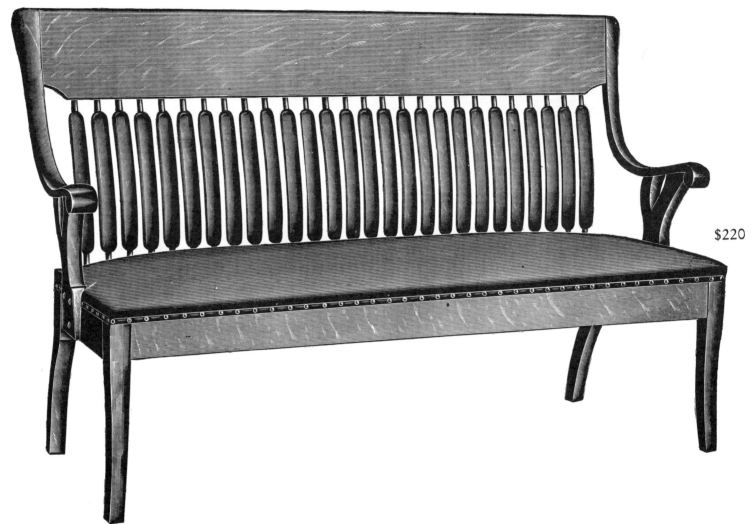

$220

No. 176½-BSUL.

Settee.
5 feet Long.
Upholstered Dark Olive Leather Spring Seat.
Golden Oak, Polished.
Weight each, 62 pounds.

$220

No. 1134-HBL.

Settee.
40 inches Long.
Upholstered Dark Olive Leather Back and Spring Seat.
Mahogany Finish, Polished.
Golden Oak, Polished.
Weight each, 40 pounds.

PHOENIX CHAIR CO.
SHEBOYGAN, WIS.

$25

No. 49.

Folding Chair.
Golden Elm, Gloss.
Weight each, 10 pounds.

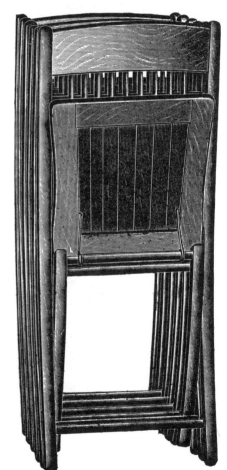

$150

No. 49.

One Half Dozen, Folded.
Golden Elm, Gloss.

PHOENIX CHAIR CO.
SHEBOYGAN, WIS.

$185

$220

No. 363-C.
Cabinet Chair.
Reversible Box.
Golden Elm, Gloss.
Weight each, 24 pounds.

No. 145.
Cabinet Chair.
Reversible Box.
Golden Elm, Gloss.
Weight each, 27 pounds.

PHOENIX CHAIR CO.
SHEBOYGAN, WIS.

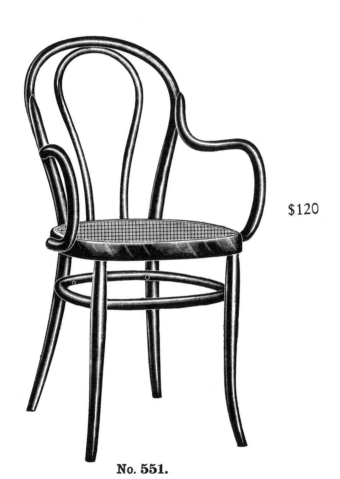

$120

$125

No. 551.

Cane Seat.
Golden Elm, Gloss.
Mahogany Finish, Polished.
Golden Oak, Polished.
Weight each, 10 pounds.

No. 551-B.

Vienna Billiard Chair.
24 inches High.
Cane Seat.
Golden Oak, Polished.
Weight each, 11 pounds.

PHOENIX CHAIR CO.
SHEBOYGAN, WIS.

$120

No. 551½.

Veneer Seat.
Golden Elm, Gloss.
Mahogany Finish, Polished.
Golden Oak, Polished.
Weight each, 10 pounds.

$125

No. 551½-B.

Vienna Billiard Chair.
24 inches High.
Veneer Seat.
Golden Oak, Polished.
Weight each, 13 pounds.

PHOENIX CHAIR CO.
SHEBOYGAN, WIS.

$175

No. 363.

Arm Chair.
Wood Seat.
Golden Elm, Gloss.
Weight each, 19 pounds.

$175

No. 363½.

Billiard Chair.
24 inches High.
Wood Seat.
Golden Elm, Gloss.
Weight each, 20 pounds.

PHOENIX CHAIR CO.
SHEBOYGAN, WIS.

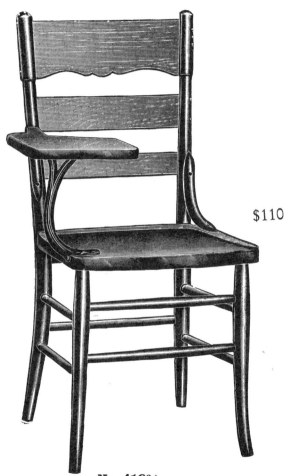

$110

No. 416¾.

University Chair.
Wood Seat.
Golden Elm, Gloss.
Weight each, 15 pounds.

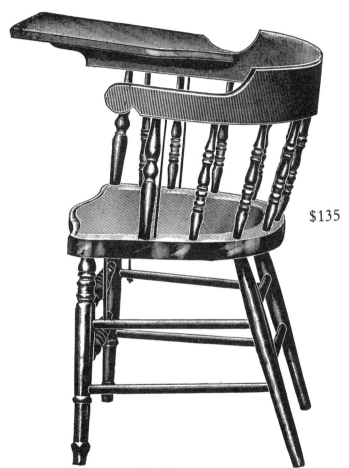

$135

No. 220.

University Chair.
Golden Elm, Gloss.
Weight each, 19 pounds.

PHOENIX CHAIR CO.
SHEBOYGAN, WIS.

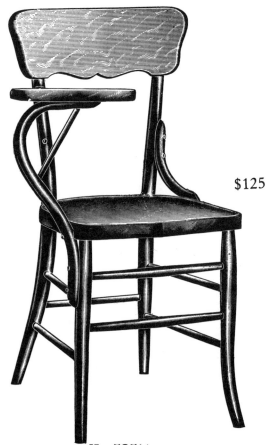

$125

No. 595½.

University Chair.
Tablet Arm.
Wood Seat.
Golden Elm, Gloss.
Weight each, 13 pounds.

$125

No. 6½.

University Chair.
Golden Elm, Gloss.
Golden Oak, Gloss.
Weight each, 15 pounds.

INDEX.